Relish
WALES

Original recipes from the region's finest chefs and restaurants. Introduction by chef Will Holland.

First Published 2016
By Relish Publications
Shield Green Farm, Tritlington,
Northumberland, NE61 3DX.

Twitter: @Relish_Cookbook
Facebook: RelishRestaurantGuide
Instagram: Relish_Cookbook
For cookbooks and recipes visit:
www.relishpublications.co.uk
For publishing enquiries visit:
www.relish-publishing.co.uk

ISBN: 978-0-9934678-3-7

Publisher: Duncan L Peters
General Manager: Teresa Peters
Design: Vicki Brown
Publishing and Marketing Executive: Rebecca Laycock
Proofing Coordinator: Valerie McLeod
Relish Photography: Andy Richardson
www.awaywithmedia.com Twitter: @andyrichardson1
Editorial Consultant: Paul Robertson
Twitter: @paulrobbo1966

Front cover photograph by: Andy Richardson

Printed in Poland on behalf of Latitude Press

Relish
PUBLICATIONS

Welcome to this third edition of Relish Wales, with a mouth-watering collection of recipes from the region's finest chefs and restaurants. We know you will enjoy cooking your way through the pages of this beautiful guide.

Since starting Relish Publications in 2009, we are privileged to have worked with hundreds of talented and highly acclaimed chefs, some of the biggest names in British food, and now have a national portfolio of over 25 regional, fine-dining guides and bespoke recipe books.

There are more than 1500 signature dishes and restaurants for you to access on our website at www.relishpublications.co.uk. We have circumnavigated the UK in our hunt for the most highly acclaimed eateries, hidden gems and those highly recommended by other top chefs in the UK.

As the proud owner of a Relish cookbook you can also subscribe for a free Relish Rewards Card which entitles members to exclusive offers at some of the featured restaurants, ranging from a bottle of Champagne to free gifts when you dine.

We love to hear from our readers! Why not post your culinary efforts on our Facebook or Instagram pages? And, if you have any questions for the chefs, email our friendly team - marketing@relishpublications.co.uk.

So, next time you're planning to dine in an outstanding restaurant or cook for friends, tantalise your tastebuds with one of our beautiful books, lie back and think of England, Scotland or Wales and enjoy planning your next meal!

Best wishes and bon appétit *Relish* x

004
CONTENTS

006
CONTENTS

009
STARTERS

Lamb with Broad Beans, Asparagus & Tarragon - **Page 172**

011
MAINS

Mascarpone Panna Cotta, Blackberries, Oats & Cucumber - Page 154

013
DESSERTS

015

FOREWORD BY WILL HOLLAND

I believe a chef is only as good as the ingredients that enter their kitchen. One of the many reasons I moved to Pembrokeshire is the truly sensational larder on the doorstep thanks to the wonderful coastline and countryside.

Not all chefs are fortunate to have the pleasure of getting their hands on fish caught metres from their kitchen door and few chefs have access to quality meat that come from the fields and woodland surrounding their restaurant. Yet I'm very lucky to have both.

From the kitchen window at Coast I can see fishing boats out in the bay, knowing their catch will be on my guests' plates later that day.

The chefs in this book benefit from similar relationships with the producers who supply their restaurants and they too have access to one of the most bountiful larders in the whole of the UK.

These chefs know the fishermen who catch their fish, the farmers who raise the animals they'll prepare, the foragers who collect their sea herbs, the gardeners who grow their vegetables and the artisan cheesemakers who make the cheese they're going to serve on their restaurant's cheeseboard.

Great ingredients don't just include prime cuts of meat, prime species of fish or other extravagant or indulgent ingredients. I'm a fan of unusual secondary cuts of meat and lesser-known species of fish. Whatever ingredients I buy, I always know the source and establish a good relationship with the supplier. If I'm using mackerel, it's been line-caught from the bay and is hours old when it comes into my kitchen.

The chefs and their teams who feature in Relish Wales Volume 3 are an exceptional group of craftsmen and women, but it is important to remember that as chefs we are merely the last people on a production line and a huge amount of hard work has already gone into the ingredients we require to do our job.

It's the farmers, fishermen, gardeners and other food producers who should take just as much credit and glory as the chefs, but who are often overlooked. These are the people who have taken the time and care to provide the raw ingredients. They are the ones who are up early milking their cows, delivering lambs in the middle of the night and risking their lives out on their fishing boats in storms.

Once a chef has the right ingredients, cooking is the easy part. A chef's responsibility is to give ingredients the respect they deserve and to prepare and cook them to the best of their ability - and of course with love.

When I opened Coast it was a blank canvas. I was in charge of a brand new, purpose-built restaurant and it was exciting to have the opportunity to put my stamp on it. Chefs are naturally creative people and there's nothing better than creating something from scratch. As a chef, freedom is one of the biggest things you can be given.

Of course not every chef has a brand new restaurant in which to cook, but every chef does have the opportunity to be creative every day, to treat each plate of food they prepare as though it was their last and to forget what happened yesterday and focus on providing excellence today. The chefs featured in Relish Wales Volume 3 all share this philosophy and I'm delighted to introduce them to you through the pages of this beautiful book.

Will Holland
Head Chef, Coast Restaurant, Saundersfoot, Pembrokeshire

016
ARBENNIG
RESTAURANT

6-10 Romilly Crescent, Cardiff, CF11 9NR

02920 341 264
www.arbennig.co.uk Twitter: @ArbennigCardiff @ChefArbennig

A rbennig is a family-owned restaurant in the trendy, leafy suburbs of Pontcanna, Cardiff. Headed by John Cook and his wife Ceri, Arbennig opened its doors in January 2014 and the pair haven't looked back since! Winning a loyal local following and a string of awards, they have even expanded to open a coffee shop/delicatessen - 'Arbennig Emporium' next door.

Arbennig means 'special' in Welsh. When asked why they chose to settle on this name for their venture, the couple explained as this is the first restaurant they have owned themselves, it is indeed special to them. Pontcanna has a large Welsh speaking community and the couple wanted to subtly fit in - as though they had always been there. We are sure you will agree that a meal enjoyed here is always very special!

The food produced in the Arbennig kitchen is of an exceptionally high quality, with a weekly changing menu that always takes advantage of the local, seasonal produce on offer. The food is never too pretentious - there is always a choice of the humble burger on offer, of course using the finest beef available from Richard Vaughan at Huntsham Farm. The setting is comfortable and friendly; relaxed fine dining for people who just enjoy good quality, real food.

Since opening in 2014, the Waitrose Good Food Guide has awarded Arbennig the highest rating of all restaurants in Cardiff. John insists the reason behind this is his passion for produce, the simplicity of his cooking and his head chef, Josie Bradshaw.

IBERICO HAM, WHITE PEACH, GORWYDD CAERPHILLY, SUTTON SOURED HONEY

SERVES 4

 Faraway Farm Chenin Blanc, 2013
(South Africa)

Ingredients

600g Iberico de Bellota
4 white peaches
400g Gorwydd Caerphilly cheese
200g wild rocket
100g Parmigiano Reggiano

Sour Honey Dressing

100g raw honey or fresh honeycomb
25ml white wine vinegar

To Serve

fresh black pepper (pinch of)

Method

Slice the Iberico ham as thinly as possible from the bone.

Cut each peach into 8 segments.

Crumble the Gorwydd Caerphilly cheese.

Wash the rocket and dry it thoroughly.

Shave the Parmigiano Reggiano using a vegetable peeler.

For The Sour Honey Dressing

Gently warm the honey in a saucepan, remove from the heat and stir in the vinegar. Allow to cool at room temperature.

To Serve

All ingredients should be served at room temperature.

Arrange all the ingredients on a plate, drizzle with the sour honey dressing and freshly cracked pepper.

Chef's Tip

This dish is all about the raw materials so buy the best that you are able to source and try not to substitute any of the ingredients to get the desired flavour combination. This is a really great summer dish and white peaches are at their best in July/August. They are a sweeter variety of peach which complements the ham and cheese perfectly.

CAMBRIAN MOUNTAIN LAMB, TOASTED BARLEY, MILK CURDS, PEAS, SALSA VERDE

SERVES 4

 Château Musar, Gaston Hochar, 2008 (Lebanon)

Ingredients

Milk Curds

1.125 litres whole milk
20ml white vinegar
salt

Toasted Barley

200g pearl barley
1 tbsp rapeseed oil
1 litre vegetable stock
½ tsp ground cumin

Peas

800g garden peas
50g butter
sea salt

Lamb

2 loins of lamb
rapeseed oil
4 sprigs fresh thyme
sea salt
cracked black pepper

Salsa Verde

mint leaves (handful of)
parsley leaves (handful of)
basil leaves (handful of)
1 tsp Dijon mustard
1 tsp capers
3 tbsp white wine vinegar
½ clove garlic
100ml rapeseed oil

To Serve

cucumber
micro leaves
frisee

muslin cloth

Method

For The Milk Curds (Prepare 24 hours ahead)

Heat the milk in a stainless steel saucepan to 80°C. Remove from the heat and add the vinegar and salt. Stir gently (don't whisk), then allow to cool. As the milk cools, you will see curds begin to form.

Wash the muslin cloth. Line the inside of a sieve with the muslin and place it over a bowl. Pour the milk curds into the cloth and leave to drain. Hang in the fridge over a bowl for 24 hours.

For The Toasted Barley

Gently fry the barley in the oil until it is golden brown and smells nutty. Cover with the vegetable stock, add the cumin and boil until tender, for about 40 minutes. Drain and allow to steam dry until cool.

For The Peas

Blanch the peas in boiling water for 30 seconds, then refresh in ice water.

Blend half the peas to a purée, then pass through a sieve, adding water if necessary. Keep the remaining peas whole.

For The Lamb

Rub the lamb with rapeseed oil and thyme. Leave at room temperature for 1 hour before cooking.

Preheat the oven to 220°C.

Season the lamb with salt and pepper. Heat a little oil in a pan and fry the lamb to seal all sides until golden brown. Remove from the pan and place in the oven for 8-12 minutes, or until the core temperature reaches 55°C. Allow to rest for at least 15 minutes.

> **Chef's Tip**
>
> Welsh lamb is a fantastic meat and you will often find it on our menu in the summer months, when the lamb has had time to mature and develop the essential fat for the best flavour.

For The Salsa Verde

Blitz all the ingredients in a blender.

To Assemble

Warm the pea purée with half the butter.

Pan fry the whole peas and pearl barley together in the remaining butter, adding salt and pepper to taste.

Carve the lamb and arrange on plate with the whole peas and barley. Scatter around the milk curds and pea purée. Garnish with seasonal leaves and finish by drizzling with salsa verde.

CHOCOLATE MOUSSE, BUTTERMILK ICE CREAM, MATCHA WHITE CHOCOLATE, PEPPERMINT

SERVES 8

 Château Haut Gléon, Carthagène Rouge, 2012 (France)

Ingredients

Chocolate Mousse

330g high quality dark chocolate
(minimum 70% cocoa solids)
10 medium free range eggs (separated)
100g caster sugar
sea salt (pinch of)

Buttermilk Ice Cream

450ml double cream
225ml whole milk
1 vanilla pod (split)
120g egg yolks (about 6 eggs)
100g caster sugar
400ml buttermilk
200g glycerin

Matcha White Chocolate

300g white chocolate (finely chopped)
1 tsp matcha green tea powder

Peppermint

200g fondant icing
1 tsp peppermint essence

Garnish

mint leaves
chocolate soil

Method

For The Chocolate Mousse (Prepare ahead)

Melt the chocolate in a bowl over simmering water and allow to cool for 10 minutes.

Whisk the egg yolks with 50g of sugar until pale and fluffy.

Place the egg whites, salt and remaining sugar in an electric mixer and whisk until soft peaks are formed.

Mix the cooled chocolate into the egg yolks. Gently fold the egg whites into the chocolate mix.

Refrigerate for 4 hours minimum.

Chef's Tip

It really is worth investing in a high quality chocolate for this dish for a superior finish - we like to use Valrhona at Arbennig.

For The Buttermilk Ice Cream

Heat the cream, whole milk and vanilla pod to 75°C.

In a separate bowl, whisk together the egg yolks and sugar.

Pour the hot milk mixture onto the egg yolks and sugar, whisking continuously. Return the mixture back to the pan and, stirring continuously on a low heat, heat to 80°C or until the custard coats the back of a spoon. Remove from the heat and leave to cool in the fridge in a clean bowl.

Once cool, remove the vanilla pod, whisk in the buttermilk and glycerin and churn in an ice cream machine.

For The Matcha White Chocolate

Melt 200g of the chocolate over simmering water to 45°C. Remove half the melted chocolate from the bowl but keep it warm.

Add the remaining chopped cold chocolate to 100g of melted chocolate and stir until the chopped chocolate is melted. Stir in the other half of the melted chocolate. Whisk in the matcha powder. Spread thinly over greaseproof paper and leave until cool and crisp.

For The Peppermint

Knead the peppermint essence into the fondant icing and roll until thin. Leave to dry uncovered. Blend in a food processor.

To Assemble

Assemble as pictured.

026
BEACH HOUSE OXWICH

Oxwich Beach, Oxwich, Swansea, SA3 1LS

01792 390 965
www.beachhouseoxwich.co.uk Twitter: @beachhouseoxwich @HGChef1

The Beach House Oxwich opened its doors in summer 2016, located on the soft, golden sands of Oxwich Bay, surrounded by magnificent coastal views.

The kitchen is led by acclaimed head chef and native Welshman Hywel Griffith, who has honed his craft at leading restaurants throughout the UK before returning to Wales. Hywel's passion for his native country means that guests can expect a menu bursting with champion ingredients from the very best Glamorgan producers and the local fishermen who land lobster on the beach right in front of the restaurant.

Dishes are prepared with skill, experience and creativity. Sample Hywel's perfectly crackled crusted bread, studded with seaweed or velvety brown crab, with flowering courgette fritter, artichoke, olive, tomato and nasturtium. For pudding try ara brith soufflé with lapsang souchong ice cream. To quench your thirst, order a signature Beach House cocktail with Brecon Five vodka, Triple Sec, mango, passion fruit and basil, or the equally quaffable non-alcoholic shaken lemonade, made with fresh lemon, rosemary and soda water. There's also a selection of craft bottled beers that come from the Gower Brewery, brewed only six miles away.

The restaurant interiors have had leading designer Martin Hulbert work his magic using a coastal palette with cushioned driftwood benches and the most comfortable, modern, leather upholstered chairs. The outside terrace, filled with potted herbs, offers the perfect place to enjoy outside dining in a most natural of seaside settings.

The Beach House prides itself on offering a relaxed dining experience with beautiful coastal views towards the renowned Three Cliffs Bay. Guests will enjoy a warm, sincere welcome, with the highest standards of service and professionalism.

BEACH HOUSE
RESTAURANT

CHARRED MACKEREL, AVOCADO, OYSTER MAYONNAISE, PASSION FRUIT

SERVES 4

 Finca Os Cobatos Godello Blanco 2014, Galicia (Spain)

Ingredients

2 mackerel

Avocado Purée

2 avocados
1 lemon (juice of)
salt (pinch of)

Oyster Mayonnaise

4 oysters
30g pasteurised egg yolks
20ml lemon juice
100ml vegetable oil

Garnish

1 Granny Smith apple
½ cucumber
12 oyster leaves
2 passion fruits
olive oil (to dress)

Method

For The Mackerel

Fillet the fish, carefully remove the gut cavity bones, then cut the fillets lengthways, removing the centre bloodline and remaining bones. Place on a lightly oiled baking tray ready to cook. Blow torch the mackerel or place under a hot grill.

> **Chef's Tip**
>
> I use a blow torch to cook the mackerel, it gives an awesome flavour!

For The Avocado Purée

Cut the avocados in half, remove the stones and skin and place the flesh in a blender. Purée with the lemon juice and season to taste. Pass through a fine *chinois*.

For The Oyster Mayonnaise

Open the oysters and place in a small pan with all the juice (be careful not to break the shell). Bring to the boil, then chill rapidly.

Place the chilled oysters and juice, yolk and lemon juice in a blender. Blend for 1 minute. Gradually, on a slow speed, add the oil.

For The Garnish

Dice the apple to 1cm cubes. Blend the trimmings and pass through a fine *chinois*. Place the apple cubes in a *sous vide* pouch and fully vacuum the apples.

For the cucumber, follow the exact same process as for the apples. If you don't have a vacuum pack machine, just keep the apples and cucumbers in their juices.

Cut the oyster leaves in half. Cut the passion fruits in half and remove all the seeds ready for plating.

To Serve

Serve as pictured, finishing with a drizzle of olive oil.

TANDOORI SPICED COD, LEEK, SPRING ONION & CAPERS

SERVES 4

 Narince, Kayra 2014 (Turkey)

Ingredients

Tandoori Spiced Cod

1kg cod
50g salt
tandoori powder (to dust)
oil (drizzle of)

Leek Purée

1kg leeks
20ml vegetable oil
salt (pinch of)
1g xanthan gum

Tandoori Butter

10g tandoori powder
100g butter
1 lemon (juice of)

Garnish

4 spring onions
capers (handful of)
oil (to fry)
200ml almond milk
2g lecithin

Method

For The Tandoori Spiced Cod

Scale the fish, remove all the bones and salt the fish for 1 hour. Wash thoroughly and pat dry. Cut the cod in to 4 pieces and dust generously with the tandoori powder. Heat a little oil in a frying pan and cook the cod, skin-side down, for 3 minutes until crispy. Turn the cod over and allow to rest for 2 minutes off the heat.

For The Leek Purée

Slice the leeks, wash thoroughly, then drain well. Place in a heavy-based pan with the oil and a pinch of salt and cook until the leeks are completely dry; the pan will catch and colour the leeks, this is perfectly fine.

Blend with the xanthan gum to help smooth and stabilise the purée. Pass through a fine *chinois*.

For The Tandoori Butter

Dry fry the spices in a hot pan, add the butter and cook to *beurre noisette*. Finish with the lemon juice.

> **Chef's Tip**
> Make sure you use a really hot pan to properly toast the spices for an authentic flavour.

For The Garnish

Thinly slice the spring onions, cover with cold water and refrigerate for 2 hours to make crisp.

Fry the drained capers in hot oil until crispy. Place on a cloth to absorb any excess oil.

Add the lecithin to the warmed almond milk, season and use a hand blender to froth.

To Serve

Place the purée into the bowls, set the cod on top, then dress with the tandoori butter and garnish.

PEACH MELBA WITH LEMON VERBENA ICE CREAM

SERVES 4

🍷 *Château de Juge Cadillac Halves 2011, Bordeaux (France)*

Ingredients

Macarons
165g icing sugar
165g ground almonds
120g egg whites
165g caster sugar

Opaline Caramel
225g sugar
35g glucose
75ml water
19g butter

Vanilla Cream
140ml semi-skimmed milk
1 vanilla pod (seeds of)
30g caster sugar
2 egg yolks
10g cornflour
75ml whipping cream

Lemon Verbena Ice Cream
330ml semi-skimmed milk
50g lemon verbena leaves
60ml double cream
35g egg yolk
78g sugar

Poached Peaches & Purée
200g sugar, 400ml water
½ vanilla pod
4 ripe peaches

Garnish
16 raspberries, biscuit crumb

4 x 55mm metal rings

Chef's Tip
For the sugar work, make sure your environment is very dry. Put a dehumidifier in your kitchen overnight. All elements can be prepared in advance.

Method

For The Macarons (Prepare ahead)
Blend the icing sugar and almonds together, then pass through a fine sieve.
Whisk the egg whites and caster sugar together to a soft peak. Fold the egg whites through the almond mix to make a smooth batter. Pipe onto greaseproof paper and allow to dry for 2 hours.
Preheat the oven to 160°C (fan).
Bake for 8-10 minutes. The macarons should still be soft in the centre.

For The Opaline Caramel
Place all the ingredients in a pan and cook to 160°C. Pour onto a tray and allow to cool. When completely cooled, blend to a fine powder. Store in an airtight container.
Preheat the oven to 120°C (fan).
Make a stencil measuring 175mm x 35mm. Position the stencil on a silicone mat and dust the sugar powder into the stencil.
Transfer to the oven for a few seconds to melt the sugar. Place the mat on a cool table for a few seconds, then wrap the caramel around a 55mm metal ring to form the shape.

For The Vanilla Cream
Bring the milk and vanilla seeds to the boil.
Beat the sugar, yolks and cornflour together, then pour the hot milk onto the egg mix and whisk thoroughly. Pour into a clean pan and cook until thick. Chill the mixture.
Whisk the cream. Beat half into the vanilla cream, then carefully fold the remainder of the cream through. Transfer the thick mixture to a piping bag.

For The Lemon Verbena Ice Cream
Boil the milk, add the lemon verbena leaves and leave to infuse until cool.
Reheat the milk, then pass through a fine sieve. Beat the yolks and sugar together, then pour the milk onto the yolks. Return to the pan and cook to 70°C. Stir in the cream and pass through a sieve again. Chill, place in a Pacojet beaker and freeze. Alternatively, churn in an ice cream machine.

For The Poached Peaches & Purée
Make a stock syrup with the sugar, water and vanilla. Drop the peaches into the stock syrup and allow to cool. Blend 2 of the peaches to make a thick, fruit purée. Peel and slice the remaining peaches.

To Serve
Drizzle the plate with peach purée. Pipe the vanilla cream into the caramel rings, top with sliced peaches, peach purée and raspberries. Top with a macaron, serving as pictured.

036
THE BLACK LION INN

Llanfaethlu, Anglesey, North Wales, LL65 4NL

01407 730 718
www.blacklionanglesey.com Twitter: @Black_Lion_Inn

The Black Lion is a renovated Grade II listed country pub restaurant based on the beautiful north coast of Anglesey. The building lay empty for over seven years before being brought back to life by local couple, Leigh and Mari Faulkner.

As a farmer's daughter, sourcing local produce is extremely important to Mari. They are extremely fortunate on Anglesey to have fantastic quality, traditional, indigenous beef, Welsh lamb, game - including pheasant and partridge, fresh fish and shellfish and artisan cheese producers right on the doorstep. They grow as much of their own herbs, salads and vegetables as possible in their garden and forage for seasonal fruits.

The Black Lion offers a simple seasonal changing menu as well as a specials board, local beer and a fantastic selection of wines. They also have two large luxurious en-suite bedrooms for guests who wish to stay the night.

Head chef Wayne Roberts is an Anglesey native who previously worked in a local country house hotel. He has a passion for seasonal, locally sourced food and enjoys the opportunity to use the best local ingredients. Wayne has been working at the Black Lion since 2014 and, during this time, they have gained an AA Rosette and have featured in the Waitrose Good Food Guide.

Head chef Wayne Roberts ensures the Black Lion Inn menu offers something for everyone - ranging from the very best of pub classics to dishes for those with more adventurous palates.

PAN FRIED SCALLOPS, ROE BUTTER, ROASTED KOHLRABI, PEA PUREE, SMOKED BACON

SERVES 4

🍷 *Silver Lake Sauvignon Blanc, 2013*
(New Zealand)

Ingredients

Roe Butter

reserved roes (from scallops)
125g salted butter (room temperature)
½ lemon (juice of)

Pea Purée

150ml double cream
100g frozen garden peas
few sprigs parsley (chopped)
½ lemon (juice of)

Roasted Kohlrabi & Bacon

1 kohlrabi
2 slices smoked bacon

Scallops

12 large scallops
oil (for frying)
salt and pepper

Method

For The Roe Butter

Place the roes in a food processor and blitz until puréed. Add the softened butter and lemon juice and mix well. Reserve in the fridge.

For The Pea Purée

Bring the cream to the boil, add the peas and simmer for 2 minutes until the peas have warmed through. Add the chopped parsley and lemon juice, then transfer to a food processor and blitz. Pass through a *chinois*.

For The Roasted Kohlrabi & Bacon

Preheat the oven to 180°C (fan).

Slice the kohlrabi into 12 thin 2½cm squares, 1cm thick. Pan fry in a little oil until golden brown, transfer to the oven and cook until *al dente*, about 10 minutes.

Julienne the bacon and place into the oven for the final 5 minutes of the kohlrabi's cooking time.

For The Scallops

While the kohlrabi bakes, heat some oil in a frying pan until it becomes slightly smoky. Reduce to a medium heat, season the scallops and place them in the pan. Leave to colour, untouched, for 1-2 minutes or until golden brown. Turn the scallops over and cook for 1 minute. Place a knob of the roe butter into the pan to glaze the scallops and cook for another minute, depending on the size of the scallops.

To Serve

Gently warm the pea purée and place a spoonful onto each plate. Arrange 3 pieces of roasted kohlrabi on top. Remove the scallops from the pan and place one on each piece of kohlrabi. Finish with the bacon on top.

> **Chef's Tip**
>
> When cooking the scallops, put oil in the pan, swirl around to coat, then tip the excess out. Too much oil will spit at you when you put the scallops in to sear. If you can't get hold of kohlrabi you can use potatoes, celeriac or any root vegetable.

BRAISED SHOULDER OF ANGLESEY LAMB, CRUSHED POTATOES, MINT OIL, HOME GROWN VEGETABLES

SERVES 4-6

Hahn Estates Central Coast Cabernet Sauvignon, California 2010 (USA)

Ingredients

Mirepoix

2 carrots
1 onion
2 sticks celery
1 leek

Braised Lamb Shoulder & Jus

2 tbsp vegetable oil
1 shoulder of lamb (boned, rolled)
1 small bunch thyme, rosemary and sage
1 bulb garlic
water (to cover)
200ml red wine
2 tbsp redcurrant jelly

Crushed Potatoes

600g Anglesey new potatoes
2 tbsp vegetable oil
125g salted Welsh butter (melted)
small bunch parsley and chives (chopped)
salt and pepper

Mint Oil

100g mint
30g icing sugar
100ml vegetable oil
seasoning

To Serve

seasonal vegetables
spinach (*blanched*, seasoned), fresh mint

Chef's Tip

The best way to crush the potatoes is by using your hands! Ensure they are clean.

Method

For The Braised Lamb Shoulder & Jus (Prepare ahead)

Preheat the oven to 220°C (fan).

Roughly chop the *mirepoix* vegetables, add the oil to coat, then roast for 20 minutes to a good colour.

Reduce the oven to 160°C (fan).

Add the lamb, herbs and garlic to the *mirepoix*. Pour in water ensuring the lamb is covered. Braise for 3-4 hours or until a knife penetrates easily with no pressure.

Remove the lamb from the water when cooked. Reduce the *liquor* to a dark colour. Cool both and refrigerate overnight.

Next day, skim the layer of fat off the jellied cooking *liquor* and discard. Bring the red wine and redcurrant jelly to the boil and reduce by half. Stir in the cooking *liquor* and simmer gently. Season to taste.

For The Crushed Potatoes

Preheat the oven to 200°C (fan).

Boil the potatoes in salted water until tender, then drain. Place on a baking tray, drizzle with oil and roast for 10 minutes until lightly golden (not essential but gives more flavour).

Allow to cool slightly, then gently crush. Stir through the melted butter and chopped herbs. Season to taste. Mould into preferred shape (baking ring optional) and place on an oiled tray.

For The Mint Oil

Blanch the mint for 2-3 minutes. Rapidly cool in ice water.

Blitz the mint and sugar using a hand blender or food processor. Gradually add in the vegetable oil and season to taste. Pass through a fine *chinois* or muslin cloth.

To Serve

Preheat the oven to 200°C (fan).

Cut the lamb in to 4-6 individual portions. Place on an ovenproof tray, add a little water, cover with foil and cook for 25 minutes. Place the potatoes in the oven for the same time.

Reheat the lamb jus by bringing to the boil. *Blanch* the vegetables in salted water for approximately 6 minutes until *al dente*.

Place some spinach in the centre of the plate and rest the lamb on top. Spoon over a some of the jus. Top with crushed potatoes and vegetables. Drizzle the mint oil around the plate and garnish with fresh mint.

LEMON & RHUBARB PANNA COTTA

SERVES 6

 Muscat de Beaumes-de-Venise, Domaine des Bernardins 2014 (France)

Ingredients

Lemon Panna Cotta

100ml whole milk
600ml double cream
200g caster sugar
2 lemons (zest and juice of)
1 lime (zest of)
3 leaves gelatine (softened)

Rhubarb Compôte

3 sticks rhubarb (washed)
300g caster sugar
3 tbsp water

Rhubarb Coulis

few spoonfuls rhubarb compôte

Rhubarb Crisps

100g caster sugar
100ml water
1 stick rhubarb (washed)

Garnish

granola
seasonal berries
fresh mint

6 jars

Method

For The Lemon Panna Cotta

Bring the milk, cream and sugar to the boil. Whisk in the zests and lemon juice. Simmer for a few minutes until slightly reduced and thickened, then turn off the heat. Add the gelatine to the warm cream mixture and whisk until well combined and dissolved. Strain and leave to cool slightly with a *cartouche* on top.

> **Chef's Tip**
>
> It's worth using whole milk as it's slightly thicker and gives a creamier consistency.

For The Rhubarb Compôte

Trim the rhubarb and cut into 2½cm pieces. Place in a saucepan with the sugar and water.

Simmer until the rhubarb is fully softened, adding more water if it starts to catch or dry out. You should end up with a thick, chunky rhubarb compôte.

For The Rhubarb Coulis

Blitz a few spoonfuls of the rhubarb compôte and pass through a fine *chinois*.

For The Rhubarb Crisps (Prepare ahead)

Preheat the oven to 100°C (fan).

Make a stock syrup with the sugar and water.

Peel the rhubarb into strips using a potato peeler. Place the strips into the boiling stock syrup for 30 seconds, then remove and place flat on a non-stick tray. Dehydrate in the oven for 4 hours.

To Assemble

Add a spoonful of rhubarb compôte in the bottom of each jar. Place in the fridge to set for 10-15 minutes. Pour over the cooled lemon cream, then return to set in the fridge for at least 2 hours.

To Serve

Place the panna cottas onto plates. Arrange a little granola to the side and top with seasonal berries and rhubarb crisps.

Add a spoonful of rhubarb coulis next to the panna cotta and, with the back of a spoon, drag the coulis across the plate.

Finish with raspberries and fresh mint.

046
BUNCH OF GRAPES

Ynysangharad Road, Mid Glamorgan, CF37 4DA

01443 402 934
www.bunchofgrapes.org.uk Twitter: @BunchGrapesCF37

Originally constructed in 1851, the Bunch of Grapes was built to supply beer by the pail to workers at the nearby famous 'Brown Lenox' Chainworks and to passing canal workers on their way from the Merthyr Iron works to Cardiff docks. As time has progressed, heavy industry has moved away but the Bunch of Grapes remains to satisfy customers' thirsts and appetites, providing food that is local, seasonal and freshly prepared.

Nick Otley gave up fashion photography and took over the Bunch of Grapes in 2000 with a vision of what the Bunch could become, born from many years eating at the now legendary Eagle on Farringdon Road, London. So he set about making it a reality and an all-consuming passion, making the most of the amazing Welsh producers, here in the heart of the valleys.

General manager Gareth Hutt, chef Rhys Coburn and Nick Otley lead a kitchen team of young chefs who are focussed on delivering quality. Provenance, sustainability and seasonality are all key principles in food philosophy as they create dishes for a menu which changes daily - dishes that are packed with flavour and served with friendly, informal service.

They are creators and passionate about everything they do, including brewing their own beers, baking fresh bread and stocking their deli with home produced goods. Becoming a centre of excellence for food and drink is their ambition, with plans in the pipeline for 2017 that include boutique bedrooms, private dining rooms and a cookery school. The Bunch has come a long way from those pails of beer.

Named as the AA Welsh Pub of the Year 2015, CAMRA Welsh Pub of the Year 2015 and making the Good Food Guide's list of Top 50 Pubs all in the same year, the Bunch of Grapes has great food and great beer in abundance, complemented by a dynamic wine menu.

CREME FRAICHE
& PICKLED
GIROLLES
£14.50

SOUFFLE

...CE BAKED
CHEESE SOUFFLE,
ROAST, PICKLED &
RAW CAULIFLOWER,
HAZELNUT PESTO
£14.00

All steaks are served
with hand cut chips

Side Orders

• ONION RINGS £...
• GRILLED WHOLE £3.50
  FIELD MUSHROOMS
• FRIED FREE 60p
  RANGE EGG
• PEPPER SAUCE £3.00
• BONE MARROW BUTTER
  £1.00
• LEMON & HERB
  BUTTER £1.00

Multiple award-winning with an honest welcome, or 'Croeso', we like to think the 'Bunch' is how a great pub and restaurant should be.

HAND-DIVED SCALLOPS, DEHYDRATED HOME CURED HAM, PEA PUREE & PICKLED SHALLOT

SERVES 4

 Saladini Pilastri, Falerio 2014 (Italy)

Ingredients

Dehydrated Ham

8 slices cured ham

Pea Purée

100g peas
20ml water
50ml double cream
salt (pinch of)
1 sprig thyme

Pickled Shallot

1 shallot (peeled)
2 lemons (juice of)

Scallops

8 hand-dived king scallops (cleaned, roe removed)
oil (to rub)
butter (knob of)

Sautéed Peas

50g fresh peas
1 tbsp butter
salt (pinch of)
½ lemon (juice of)

Method

For The Dehydrated Ham (Prepare ahead)

Lay the ham flat on a tray and place in a dehydrator for 24-48 hours or until crisp. Alternatively, bake at 100-120°C for 1-2 hours.

For The Pea Purée

Place all the ingredients in a saucepan. Cover with a lid and cook for 2-3 minutes. Blitz until smooth then pass through a fine sieve. Cool over ice to ensure the purée stays green.

For The Pickled Shallot

Slice the shallot into very thin rings. Squeeze lemon juice onto the rings and leave to pickle for 90 minutes.

For The Scallops

Heat a large frying pan until lightly smoking. Oil the scallops and place them in the pan. Cook until well coloured on both sides, turning just once. Finish with foaming butter.

Chef's Tip

Oil the scallop, not the pan. Always use hand-dived scallops - they're more expensive but far better quality.

For The Sautéed Peas

Blanch the peas in boiling, salted water for 30 seconds. Heat a saucepan with the butter, add the peas and seasoning. Cook for 1-2 minutes, finishing with lemon juice.

To Assemble The Dish

Plate as pictured, making sure you cook the scallops at the last minute.

BREAST OF CEFNLLAN FARM DUCK, DUCK LEG BONBON, PRESSED POTATO TERRINE, PICKLED CHERRIES & PUREE

SERVES 4

🍷 *St John's Road Motley Bunch, Grenache, Mataro, Shiraz 2013 (Australia)*

Ingredients

Pickled Cherries

3 black peppercorns
200ml white wine vinegar
100ml white wine
40g sugar
2 tbsp grenadine
½ orange (zest of)
12 whole cherries

Potato Terrine

3 large, waxy potatoes
150ml chicken stock
1 clove garlic
1 small bunch thyme

Duck Bonbons

1 cooked duck leg
1 tsp fennel seeds
1 tbsp lemon zest
100g mashed potato
2 egg yolks
salt (pinch of)
flour, 1 egg (beaten) panko (to *pane*)

Duck

1 tbsp oil
4 duck breasts
salt and pepper

Cherry Purée

100g cherries (stalks and stones removed)
2 tbsp grenadine
water (dash of)

baking tray (greased, lined)

Method

For The Pickled Cherries (Prepare ahead)

Place the pickling ingredients in a saucepan, heating until the sugar has dissolved. When cooled, pour over the cherries and leave to marinate for 24 hours.

For The Potato Terrine (Prepare ahead)

Preheat the oven to 200ºC.

Grate the potatoes into a cloth and squeeze out any juice. Infuse the stock with the garlic and thyme for 5-10 minutes. Place the grated potato in the prepared baking tray. Pour the stock through a sieve over the potatoes. Press well and bake for 25-30 minutes. Once cooked, lay a heavy weight on top to keep pressed. Trim and cut into rectangles when cooled. When serving, oil the rectangles and bake until warmed through.

For The Duck Bonbons (Prepare ahead)

Shred the cooked duck leg into a mixing bowl with the fennel seeds, lemon, potato and yolks. Season well and mix together. Shape into balls and set in the fridge. Once set, *pane* with the flour, egg and breadcrumbs. Deep fry (190ºC) for about 3 minutes until golden and crispy.

> **Chef's Tip**
>
> Using panko instead of plain breadcrumbs gives extra crispness to the bonbons.

For The Duck

Preheat the oven to 200ºC.

Heat the oil in a large frying pan. Place the duck in, skin-side down, and season. When coloured, flip and place in the oven for 8-10 minutes. After roasting, leave to rest for 4-5 minutes in a warm place.

For The Cherry Purée

Add the cherries to a saucepan with the grenadine and water. Cook until soft. Blitz well and pass through a sieve.

To Assemble The Dish

Plate as pictured.

LIME & GINGER PANNA COTTA, CHILLED RHUBARB CONSOMME, CRYSTALLISED GINGER

SERVES 4

🍷 *Otley Brewing Co, Thai Bo, Lime Leaf, Lemongrass & Thai Ginger Pale Ale (UK)*

Ingredients

Lime & Ginger Panna Cotta

700ml double cream
1 lime (zest of)
1 thumb ginger (roughly chopped)
4 leaves gelatine (soaked in cold water)
250g caster sugar

Rhubarb Consommé

4 large rhubarb stalks (roughly chopped)
1 thumb ginger
50ml grenadine
400ml water
1 lemon (juice and zest of)
1 orange (juice and zest of)

Poached Rhubarb

200ml water
50ml grenadine
100g granulated sugar
1 rhubarb stalk (cut into small cubes)

Garnish

12 cubes crystallised ginger

4 panna cotta moulds

Method

For The Lime & Ginger Panna Cotta

Infuse the cream with lime zest and ginger on a low heat for 30 minutes. Drain the gelatine and add to the warm cream, whisking until dissolved. Add the sugar and pass through a sieve. Pour into the moulds and set in the fridge for 2-3 hours.

Chef's Tip

The longer you infuse the lime and ginger, the deeper the flavour becomes. To demould the panna cotta, place into hot water for 5-10 seconds and then turn upside down.

For The Rhubarb Consommé

Heat the rhubarb, ginger, grenadine and water to 75°C. Remove from the heat and add the orange and lemon juice and zest. Leave to infuse for 2-3 hours in the fridge.

For The Poached Rhubarb

Heat the water with the grenadine and sugar to 60°C. Pour over the diced rhubarb and set aside. Chill.

To Assemble The Dish

Serve as pictured and garnish with the crystallised ginger cubes.

056
COAST RESTAURANT

Coppet Hall Beach, Saundersfoot, Pembrokeshire, SA69 9AJ

01834 810 800
www.coastsaundersfoot.co.uk Twitter: @CoastRestaurant @ChefWillH

With stunning views across one of the prettiest bays in Wales and sensational food cooked by one of the UK's finest chefs - Coast has it all!

In the short time since opening, Coast has achieved a number of accolades, including winning the coveted AA Restaurant of the Year for Wales in 2016. This success is down to the hard work of chef Will Holland, his wife Kamila who manages the restaurant and their loyal kitchen and front of house teams.

Will developed his skills working in various Michelin starred restaurants and hotels around the UK. He won a Michelin star of his own when he was just 29 and gained a prestigious Acorn Award as one of the food industry's highest achievers under the age of 30. In 2016, Will was named UK Restaurant Chef of the Year by The Craft Guild of Chefs in their annual awards, often dubbed 'the chefs' Oscars'.

Coast has given Will the opportunity to combine the technique and consistency he learned at his previous fine dining establishments with the informality that a bright and airy, seaside, 'fish-centric' restaurant brings. Service is friendly and attentive, even though the restaurant can be busy with up to 200 covers a day.

"Coast is a great place to be" says Will. "The restaurant must have one of the best views in the UK, as well as access to some of the finest produce. We're surrounded by land and sea with suppliers on our doorstep. From my kitchen window I can see my lobster fisherman pulling up his pots in the bay."

Little wonder Will and his team are enthralled by working at Coast. Their passion is also shared by a discerning and loyal clientele.

"As a chef, I see it as my responsibility to give ingredients the respect they deserve. I prepare and cook them to the best of my ability - and, of course, with love." Chef Will Holland

SEARED SCALLOPS, CONFIT PORK BELLY, CAULIFLOWER, LIME SYRUP, PICKLED RAISINS, CRISPY CAPERS

SERVES 4

 Weingut Rabl, Grüner Veltliner 'Langenlois' Kamptal 2015 (Austria)

Ingredients

Pork Belly
500g whole pork belly (boneless, skinless)
50g sea salt crystals

Cauliflower Garnishes
1 cauliflower
125g butter

Pickled Raisins
28 raisins
150ml sherry vinegar

Lime Syrup
9 limes (juice and fine zest of)
50ml light olive oil
50g caster sugar

Crispy Capers
28 large capers (deep fried at 175°C until crispy)

Tempura Batter
50g plain flour
35g cornflour
10g baking powder
sparkling water (to mix)

Scallops
8 medium size scallops (diver-caught)
50ml light olive oil

Chef's Tip
This dish is just as delicious with or without either the scallops or the pork belly. The combination of the garnishes works well with scallops or pork belly on their own, so don't feel you have to serve both together.

Method

For The Pork Belly (Prepare 48 hours ahead)

Rub a third of the salt on the flesh side and the remainder on the fat side of the belly. Leave for 24 hours.

Preheat the oven to 90°C (fan).

Wash off the excess salt, pat dry and place in a roasting tray. Cover with tin foil and transfer to the oven for 10 hours. Remove from the oven and set another roasting tray on top. Place in the fridge to press. When completely chilled, cut four 1cm thick slices.

For The Cauliflower Garnishes

Cut four 2mm thick slices of cauliflower directly through the middle of the cauliflower and reserve until required.

Cut 12 small florets, *blanch* in boiling, salted water for 1 minute and reserve until required. Roughly chop the remaining cauliflower. Place the butter in a saucepan and heat over a medium heat until it turns 'nut brown' in colour. Add the chopped cauliflower to the pan and cook over a low heat for 20–30 minutes until caramelised and completely soft. Transfer to a liquidiser and blend until smooth. Keep warm.

For The Pickled Raisins

Bring the raisins and vinegar to the boil. Remove from the heat and allow to cool.

For The Lime Syrup

Warm the lime zest and oil in a pan to 40°C.

Reduce the lime juice and sugar over a medium heat to 100ml. Off the heat, slowly whisk in the oil until *emulsified*.

For The Tempura Batter

Mix all the ingredients with enough sparkling water to form a batter. Coat the *blanched* cauliflower florets in the batter and deep fry at 175°C for 1-2 minutes until crispy and golden.

To Cook The Scallops & Assemble The Dish

Heat a heavy-based frying pan until hot. Add the oil followed by the pork belly slices. Fry for 1 minute on each side or until caramelised. Remove from the pan and keep warm. Add the cauliflower slices to the hot pan and fry for 1 minute on each side or until caramelised. Remove from the pan and keep warm. Add the scallops to the hot pan and sear for 1 minute on each side or until caramelised. Remove from the pan and serve immediately.

Swirl the lime syrup on the plate and arrange the elements as pictured.

GINGERBREAD CRUSTED JOHN DORY, BRAISED WHITE BEANS, CHARGRILLED GRELOT ONIONS & ARTICHOKES, SAFFRON EMULSION

SERVES 4

Petritis, Kyperounda Winery 2015
Limassol (Cyprus)

Ingredients

Gingerbread

25g candied stem ginger
100g golden syrup
60g soft dark brown sugar
125g self-raising flour
10g ground ginger
2g bicarbonate of soda
1 large egg
70ml whole milk

Braised White Beans

150g dried white beans
1 litre fish stock

Saffron Emulsion

1 large Maris Piper potato (baked for 1 hour)
45ml whole milk
saffron (pinch of)
¼ clove garlic
2 egg yolks
50ml light olive oil
salt, lemon juice (spritz of)
cayenne pepper (to taste)

Grelot Onions & Artichokes

8 grelot onions
4 globe artichoke hearts (cooked)

John Dory Fillets

4 x 150g John Dory fillets (skinless)
50ml light olive oil

27cm x 7cm x 7cm tin (lined with silicone paper)

Method

For The Gingerbread

Preheat the oven to 150°C (fan).
Finely grate the stem ginger and place in a saucepan with the syrup and sugar. Warm until the sugar has dissolved. Transfer to an electric mixer and add the remaining ingredients. Beat well before transferring to the prepared tin. Bake for 45 minutes.
Allow to cool before roughly chopping and leaving to dry. Once it is completely dry, place in a food processor and blend to a crumb.

> **Chef's Tip**
> If you don't have time to make the gingerbread, try crushing shop bought ginger snap biscuits and using them as an alternative – it works equally well.

For The Braised White Beans (Prepare ahead)

Soak the beans in cold water for 24 hours.
Drain from the water and place in a saucepan with the stock. Bring to the boil, reduce the heat and simmer gently for 1 hour or until tender.

For The Saffron Emulsion

Scoop the flesh out of the potato and weigh 60g. Warm the milk and saffron in a saucepan. Place the warmed milk, potato flesh, garlic and egg yolks in a liquidiser. Blend until smooth before gradually adding the oil. Season to taste with salt, cayenne pepper and lemon juice.

For The Grelot Onions & Artichokes

Blanch the onions in boiling, salted water for 2 minutes. Refresh in ice water and reserve until required. When ready to serve, cut each artichoke heart in half and lightly chargrill with the grelot onions.

To Cook The John Dory Fillets

Preheat a large, heavy-based frying pan until hot. Add the oil followed by the John Dory fillets. Fry for 2-3 minutes on each side until caramelised. Remove from the pan, sprinkle generously with gingerbread crumb and keep warm.

To Assemble The Dish

Flick the saffron *emulsion* over each plate. Scatter the white beans over, add 2 chargrilled onions, 2 half artichoke hearts, 1 gingerbread crusted John Dory fillet and a pinch of gingerbread crumb to each plate. Serve immediately.

LIQUORICE PANNA COTTA, CHOCOLATE & BEETROOT BROWNIE, POACHED BLACKCURRANTS, BEETROOT ICE CREAM

SERVES 4

 *Quady Winery, Elysium Black Muscat 2014
California (USA)*

Ingredients

Liquorice Panna Cotta

170ml double cream
60ml whole milk
60g sugar
5g liquorice essence
1 leaf gelatine (soaked in cold water)

Chocolate & Beetroot Brownie

2 large eggs
125g sugar
40ml maple syrup
125g 70% dark chocolate (melted)
125g raw beetroot (coarsely grated)
40g plain flour
2 tsp baking powder
15g cocoa powder
25g ground almonds
50ml espresso
15ml vegetable oil

Poached Blackcurrants

200g blackcurrants
25g sugar

Beetroot Ice Cream

325g raw beetroot (finely chopped)
500ml whole milk
75ml whipping cream
5 egg yolks
100g sugar

Garnish

baby coriander cress

27cm x 7cm x 7cm tin (lined with silicone paper)
4 small, round moulds

Method

For The Liquorice Panna Cotta (Prepare ahead)

Warm all the ingredients, except the gelatine, in a saucepan.

Squeeze the gelatine and add to the pan to dissolve. Divide the mixture between the 4 moulds and place in the fridge to set for 2-3 hours.

For The Chocolate & Beetroot Brownie

Preheat the oven to 150°C (fan).

Using an electric mixer, whisk the eggs, sugar and maple syrup until light and fluffy. Add the remaining ingredients and beat well. Transfer to the prepared tin and bake for 40 minutes. Allow to cool before breaking into rough chunks.

> **Chef's Tip**
>
> The brownie on its own makes a lovely treat to serve with coffee after dinner. The beetroot in it adds a great natural sweetness to balance the bitter chocolate flavour.

For The Poached Blackcurrants

Gently cook the blackcurrants and sugar in a saucepan over a low heat until tender but still retaining their shape. Set aside in their juice and allow to cool.

For The Beetroot Ice Cream

Place the beetroot in a saucepan with the milk. Cover with a lid and simmer until the beetroot is tender. Strain the cooked beetroots and transfer them to a liquidiser with 200ml of the cooking *liquor*. Blend to a smooth purée. Pour the remaining cooking *liquor* into a saucepan with the cream and bring to the boil. Place the egg yolks and sugar in a bowl and mix. Gradually add the boiling liquid, whisking continuously. Return the mixture to the pan and cook gently over a low heat, stirring continuously until the mix thickens slightly and reaches 80°C. Check this temperature using a digital temperature probe. Remove from the heat and add the beetroot purée. Churn in an ice cream machine. Freeze until required.

To Assemble The Dish

Swirl some of the blackcurrant juice around each plate. Remove the panna cottas from the moulds and place one on each plate along with a spoonful of blackcurrants, 5 chunks of brownie, a sprinkling of brownie crumbs and 5 sprigs of coriander cress. Finish each dish with a scoop of beetroot ice cream. Serve immediately.

EPICURE BY RICHARD DAVIES

Celtic Manor Resort, Coldra Woods, Newport, NP18 1HQ

01633 410 262
www.celtic-manor.com/epicure Twitter: @TheCelticManor

E picure (noun): person of refined taste who takes particular pleasure in fine food and drink.

If ever a restaurant lived up to its name it is Epicure by Richard Davies, the fine dining experience created at the Celtic Manor Resort.

One of two Signature restaurants at the resort, Epicure's exquisite and carefully crafted menu is sure to impress the most discerning of gourmets. The restaurant offering reflects seasonality with a strong commitment to the use of locally sourced ingredients, producing fresh, intense flavours for an unforgettable dining experience.

Epicure represents a coming home for Richard who worked in the kitchens at Celtic Manor as a teenager when the Resort Hotel opened back in 1999, before climbing the culinary ladder at some leading restaurants including the 3 Michelin starred Gordon Ramsay in London. He has since gained Michelin stars of his own in his two previous head chef posts at Sawyards in West Sussex, and the Manor House at Castle Combe, before returning home to Wales to establish the new fine dining offering at Celtic Manor.

Situated just off the opulent marbled lobby of the Resort Hotel, Epicure's cascading crystal chandeliers and walnut floorboards create a stunning, modern ambience in which to savour a sumptuous fine dining occasion.

"It's a beautiful dining room and Celtic Manor is a stunning hotel," says Richard. "I knew I was coming back to the best hotel in Wales and now I want to give it the best restaurant in Wales. I like to choose the best quality ingredients - local where possible - and use modern techniques to create a memorable and exciting dining experience for guests."

Along with à la carte menus for lunch and dinner, there is also an exquisite six course evening tasting menu for diners wishing to share the ultimate gastronomic experience at this 3 AA Rosette restaurant.

The Epicure offering reflects seasonality with a strong commitment to the use of locally sourced ingredients, producing fresh, intense flavours for an unforgettable dining experience.

CITRUS CURED SALMON, HORSERADISH PANNA COTTA, BEETROOT & ORANGE

SERVES 4

 Canto Real Verdejo 2012, Rueda (Spain)

Ingredients

Citrus Cured Salmon

500g salmon
100g caster sugar
100g table salt
1 lemon (zest and juice of)
1 orange (zest and juice of)
1 pink grapefruit (zest and juice of)
1 lime (zest and juice of)

Pickled Beetroot

1 large beetroot
150ml pomace oil
3 tbsp white wine vinegar
3 tbsp honey
1½ tbsp sugar
1 sprig thyme

Beetroot Emulsion

400ml beetroot juice
80ml red wine vinegar
2 egg yolks
300ml sunflower oil
salt (to taste)

Horseradish Panna Cotta

100ml whole milk
100ml double cream
freshly grated horseradish (to taste)
salt (pinch of)
1 leaf gelatine (soaked in cold water)

Garnish

1 large orange (seedless)
bronze fennel
borage flowers
watercress

Method

For The Citrus Cured Salmon (Prepare ahead)

Skin the salmon, or ask your fishmonger to do this for you, and make sure there are no pin bones left in it. Mix the sugar and salt evenly and sprinkle on a flat tray. Using a fine grater, zest the citrus fruits and mix well. Sprinkle half over the salt and sugar mix. Place the salmon on top and sprinkle a good layer of the salt mix over it, then add the remaining zest. Juice the fruits and pour lightly over the salmon. Cover and place in the fridge. Turn the fish after 3 hours, leave for another 3 hours, then wash thoroughly and dry well with a clean tea towel or paper towel. Leave to firm in the fridge for at least an hour before use.

> **Chef's Tip**
>
> The salmon can be cured in advance to save preparation time on the day.

For The Pickled Beetroot (Prepare ahead)

Peel the beetroot and slice thinly on a mandoline. Add all the ingredients, except the thyme, into a container and *emulsify*. Add the thyme leaves and pour over the beetroot, then marinate overnight.

For The Beetroot Emulsion

Reduce the beetroot juice to 80ml and leave to cool. Add the vinegar and egg yolks, then slowly whisk in the oil to *emulsify*. Season with salt to taste.

For The Horseradish Panna Cotta (Prepare ahead)

Boil the milk and cream, then grate in the horseradish to your desired taste, season and pass through a fine sieve. Add the gelatine then pour into a tray and leave to set in the fridge until needed.

To Assemble

Dice the salmon into 2½cm pieces (they do not have to be a perfect shape, they will still taste just as great) and assemble on the plate. Peel and segment the orange and arrange around the salmon. Using a bottle or piping bag, dot the beetroot *emulsion* around the plate. Add the pickled beetroot, spoon around the panna cotta and dress with the fresh herbs and flowers.

WELSH LAMB, CAULIFLOWER, CHOCOLATE & GOLDEN RAISINS

SERVES 4

Albert Bichot, Bourgogne Vieilles Vignes, de Pinot Noir, 2013 (France)

Ingredients

Lamb Rump
4 x 225g Welsh lamb rumps (excess fat and sinew removed)
extra virgin olive oil
4 sprigs fresh thyme
4 sprigs fresh rosemary
rapeseed oil (dash of)

Chocolate Jelly
230ml chicken stock
80g bitter chocolate (chopped, plus extra for grating)
3g agar agar

Cauliflower Purée
50g butter
½ onion (finely sliced)
1 clove garlic (finely sliced)
1 cauliflower (washed, sliced)
200ml chicken stock, 300ml double cream

Caramelised Cauliflower
1 cauliflower (washed)
25g butter, salt, pepper

Vinaigrette
60ml good quality white wine vinegar
240ml extra virgin olive oil, salt (to taste)

Cauliflower Couscous
rapeseed oil
30g pancetta (finely diced)
1 cauliflower (washed, grated)
1 pinch chives (chopped), salt
100g golden raisins (soaked in boiling water for 20-30 minutes)

To Serve
2 baby globe artichokes (cooked)
extra virgin olive oil, salt
100ml lamb jus (warmed)
sorrel (2½ handfuls of)

Method

For The Lamb Rump (Prepare ahead)
Marinate the lamb rumps in the oil and herbs for at least 24 hours. Cook in a water bath at 57°C for 1 hour. Remove from the water bath and vac pack bag and dry off any excess moisture with kitchen paper. Seal in a hot pan with a small dash of rapeseed oil until golden brown on all sides, remove and place on a board ready to carve.

Alternatively, caramelise the rumps in a pan and put in the oven at 180°C for around 8 minutes, then leave to rest for 5 minutes.

For The Chocolate Jelly
Heat the chicken stock in a small saucepan until it reaches a simmer, then add the chocolate and whisk to melt. Mix thoroughly and leave to cool. Gently whisk in the agar agar, bring to the boil while stirring, then pour into a shallow tray. Allow to cool and place in the fridge to set while you prepare the other elements.

> **Chef's Tip**
> You can source the agar agar online.

For The Cauliflower Purée
Melt the butter in a heavy-based saucepan over a medium heat. Add the onion and garlic and cook until soft and golden brown. Add the sliced cauliflower, cook until golden and caramelised, then add the stock. Bring to a simmer and cook until the cauliflower is soft and tender. Continue to simmer until the stock reduces by half. Add the cream and reduce by half again, remove from the heat and transfer to a blender. Blitz until smooth, pass through a fine strainer and set aside until required.

For The Caramelised Cauliflower
Cut the cauliflower into medium-sized florets and *blanch* in salted, boiling water until tender, for approximately 2-3 minutes. Strain and cool in ice water, then drain well and set aside. Add the butter to a frying pan and make a very light *beurre noisette*. Add the florets, caramelise until golden brown and season.

For The Vinaigrette
Whisk together all the ingredients and set aside.

For The Cauliflower Couscous
Place a saucepan over a medium heat and add a small dash of oil. Once the oil is hot, add the pancetta and fry until caramelised. Add the grated cauliflower, season to taste and finish with a good pinch of chives. Finally, add the raisins and a dash of the vinaigrette to taste.

To Serve
Pan fry the baby artichoke globes in a little olive oil and season. Slice each rump into 3 pieces and serve as pictured.

MILLIONAIRE'S TART

SERVES 4

🍷 *Elysium Black Muscat, Mont Tauch Maury
Reserve, California 2011 (USA)*

Ingredients

Sweet Pastry

240g butter
170g icing sugar
1½ medium eggs
1 lemon (zest of)
1 vanilla pod (seeds of)
515g plain flour

Salted Caramel

250g caster sugar
350ml double cream
2 leaves gelatine (soaked in cold water)
salt (to taste)

Chocolate Mousse

250g dark chocolate
150ml double cream
150g egg white
salt (pinch of)

Crème Fraîche Ice Cream

2 egg yolks
60g sugar
125ml whole milk
125g crème fraîche

Chocolate Crumb

100g sugar
100g almonds
600g plain flour
25g cocoa powder
salt (pinch of)
50g butter (melted)

To Serve

gold leaf (optional)

4 individual tart cases

Method

For The Sweet Pastry

Cream the butter and icing sugar in a mixing bowl until light and fluffy. Add the eggs bit by bit, then add the lemon zest and vanilla seeds. Add the flour and mix thoroughly. Press flat between greaseproof paper and set in the fridge until firm.

Preheat the oven to 180°C (fan).

Roll the pastry out thinly and line the tart cases, trimming off any excess pastry around the top. Line with cling film and fill with rice, then blind bake for 6-8 minutes or until the pastry starts to firm around the top. Remove the rice and cling film, turn the heat down to 160°C (fan) and bake for a further 8-10 minutes or until firm, golden and crisp. Set aside to cool until serving.

For The Salted Caramel

Place the sugar in a non-stick pan and put on a medium to high heat to caramelise until golden, keep stirring the sugar as it melts. Once golden, add the cream and dissolve all the sugar over the heat. Squeeze any water from the gelatine and add to the caramel. Season with salt and refrigerate until needed.

For The Chocolate Mousse

Melt the chocolate and cream in a bowl over simmering water. When melted, whisk in the egg white, add a pinch of salt, then charge in a cream whipper gun. Keep warm until needed, for a maximum of 2 hours. Alternatively, you can use a traditional chocolate mousse, but this will not give the same effect.

For The Crème Fraîche Ice Cream

Place the yolks and sugar into a bowl and whisk to mix. Bring the milk and crème fraîche to the boil and pour over the egg mix, whisking to incorporate. Cook gently for 3-4 minutes over a medium heat. Leave to cool, then churn in an ice cream machine.

For The Chocolate Crumb

Preheat the oven to 160°C (fan).

Mix all the dry ingredients thoroughly, then add the melted butter. Spread the crumb onto a baking tray with greaseproof paper and bake for 15 minutes, turning halfway.

To Assemble

Pipe or spoon the caramel into the bottom of the tart cases, then gently fill the tart case with chocolate mousse. Ball the ice cream and place in the centre (we wrap ours in gold leaf), sprinkle with the chocolate crumb and serve.

> **Chef's Tip**
> This dish can be adapted with different flavours, try cherry compôte with pistachio ice cream.

THE FALCONDALE HOTEL & RESTAURANT

Falcondale Drive, Lampeter, Ceredigion, SA48 7RX

01570 422 910
www.thefalcondale.co.uk Twitter: @thefalcondale

Hidden within the luscious Teifi Valley in 14 acres of woodlands and lovingly cared for gardens, is the Italianate-styled Grade II listed Falcondale, a 4 star country house hotel.

Owners Chris and Lisa Hutton have restored the hotel to its former glory, offering luxury in a relaxed home-from-home atmosphere. From a roaring log fire to a Pimms and afternoon tea on the sunny terrace, the attentive and professional team are there to make your stay the first of many.

The restaurant has been awarded 2 AA Rosettes for nine consecutive years, offering indulgence in a relaxed atmosphere, with head chef Alex Rees and his team using the finest local produce, such as seafood caught in Cardigan Bay just 20 miles from the hotel. Let them expand your taste buds with their handcrafted wine list, chosen by Lisa, to enhance each bite of your devotedly prepared meal.

Bring along your best four-legged friend, as the Falcondale has been voted one of six best dog friendly hotels in the UK by the Daily Mail. With a blanket, homemade biscuits, dinner or a pampered pooch box, your dog will be lord of the manor.

Set in the beautiful Ceredigion countryside you'll be blown away by the landscape with the rugged Cambrian Mountains on one side and the Cardigan coastline just a stone's throw away on the other.

From dinner in a luxurious candlelit restaurant to delicious afternoon tea filled with homemade cakes and treats, the Falcondale team will make each visit as special and exciting as the first.

CRAB WITH PINEAPPLE & WATERMELON

SERVES 4

🍷 *Gewürztraminer Réserve 2013, Cave de Turckheim, Alsace (France)*

Method

For The Pineapple Purée

Place the pineapple, pineapple juice and a splash of vinegar in a pan and bring to the boil. Simmer until the liquid has reduced by half. Transfer to a blender and blitz until smooth.

Chill until needed.

For The Crab

Mix together the crab, mayonnaise, chilli, coriander and a pinch of salt.

> **Chef's Tip**
> Use hand-picked fresh crab meat for the best flavour.

To Assemble The Dish

Place the watermelon rectangles in the centre of your plate and place a large *quenelle* of the crab on top. Dot the pineapple purée around the plate and garnish with edible flowers.

Ingredients

Pineapple Purée

1 pineapple (peeled, diced)
300ml pineapple juice
white wine vinegar (splash of)

Crab

400g hand-picked white crab meat
50g mayonnaise
1 bird's eye chilli (finely chopped)
small bunch coriander (finely chopped)
salt (pinch of)

Garnish

½ watermelon (cut into rectangles)
edible flowers

DUCK BREAST WITH POMMES MAXINE & PORT JELLY

SERVES 4

 Kim Crawford Pinot Noir, 2014, Marlborough (New Zealand)

Ingredients

4 duck breasts

Veal Jus

1kg veal bones
water (to cover)
1 tsp gravy browning
1 tbsp redcurrant jelly

Port Jelly

300ml port jelly
1 tsp sugar
1½g agar agar

Diced Beetroot & Beetroot Foam

500g table salt
3 fresh beetroot (trimmed)
double cream (dash of)

Pommes Maxine

4 large potatoes (sliced wafer thin)
butter (knob of)

To Serve

4 chantenay carrots (cut into chunks, *blanched*)
1 Romanesco (cut into florets, *blanched*)

4 metal ramekins or dishes

Method

For The Veal Jus (Prepare ahead)

Preheat the oven to 250°C (fan).

Brown the bones in the oven for 45 minutes. Place the bones in a stock pan and cover with water. Bring to the boil and simmer for 8 hours, scooping off any surface scum with a spoon. Remove the bones and retain the liquid. Boil the liquid and reduce by two thirds, to about 500ml. Add the gravy browning and redcurrant jelly.

For The Port Jelly

Boil the port and sugar in a pan and reduce by half before whisking in the agar agar. Pour the liquid in a suitable container for cooling and refrigerate. Once cold and set, cut the jelly into small cubes, about 1-1½cm.

For The Diced Beetroot & Beetroot Foam

Preheat the oven to 160°C (fan).

Sprinkle the salt on a metal tray and place the beetroot on top Bake for 1 hour. When cooked through, peel and dice the beetroot. Transfer one third of the beetroot into a blender with a dash of cream and a pinch of salt. Blitz to a smooth purée. When cool, place into an espuma gun.

Chef's Tip

Instead of an espuma gun, you can use a hand blender to whisk the liquid and spoon the foam off the top.

For The Pommes Maxine

Preheat the oven to 160°C (fan).

Layer the potatoes into the individual ramekins or dishes. *Clarify* the butter over a gentle heat and pour on top of the potatoes. Bake in the oven for 30 minutes, or until tender. Carefully turn the potatoes out onto a towel covered board.

For The Duck

Place the breasts, skin-side down, in a cold pan and cook slowly until the skin is crispy. Turn the breasts over and cook for 1 minute. Remove from the pan and leave to rest for 10 minutes, then slice.

To Assemble

Plate the potatoes and top with the sliced duck breast.

Arrange the Romanesco, carrots and diced beetroot around the outside of the plate. Add 3 pieces of diced port jelly. Gently heat the veal jus and drizzle over the dish. Finish with the beetroot foam.

POACHED PEACH WITH SHORTBREAD CRUMB

SERVES 4

Araldica Classici Moscato Passito 'Palazzina'
2012, Araldica Vini Piemontesi, Piemonte (Italy)

Ingredients

Poached Peaches

200ml water
200ml sugar
4 ripe peaches (whole, cored)

Shortbread Crumb

250g butter
110g caster sugar
360g plain flour

To Serve

vanilla ice cream
fresh berries (selection of)
peach jelly (cubed)
micro mint leaves

Method

For The Poached Peaches

Bring the water and sugar to the boil and add the peaches. Simmer for around 15 minutes until the peaches are soft. Drop the peaches into ice cold water and peel. Leave the peaches to cool. Reduce the *liquor* in the pan by half to form a glaze.

> **Chef's Tip**
>
> You can use nectarines in place of peaches: it's important that they are ripe.

For The Shortbread Crumb

Preheat the oven to 150°C (fan).

Cream the butter and sugar together. Mix in the flour and bring together into a ball. Roll out to the thickness of a pound coin and cut into even sized pieces. Place onto baking parchment on a baking sheet and bake for 15 minutes until a light golden brown. When cool, crumble it using your fingers.

To Assemble

Spoon the shortbread crumb onto the plate. Pipe the vanilla ice cream into the core of the peaches and place on top of the crumb. Spoon a little of the glaze over each peach so that they shine. Garnish with seasonal berries.

086
THE GALLERY

2 Broad Street, Barry, Vale of Glamorgan, CF62 7AA

01446 735 300
www.the-gallery-restaurant.co.uk Twitter: @TheGalleryBarry

Chef proprietor Barnaby Hibbert and family opened The Gallery in 2013. The building constructed in the Edwardian times has been sympathetically renovated and restored, ensuring the restaurant retains many of its fine architectural features from the era but also feels very modern.

The first floor restaurant features chunky wooden tables, an open kitchen, original fireplace and two period chandeliers. The ground floor bar dispenses carefully crafted cocktails, Welsh beer, it has a dark wooden floor, with a wood burner, concrete bar and exposed brick wall. There is also a south facing courtyard garden space for the summer.

With a monthly changing, concise, seasonal menu, The Gallery prides itself on sourcing the finest local ingredients and turning them into beautiful dishes of clear, harmonious flavours with modern twists on classic themes.

Expert foragers scour the countryside and seashore in and around the vale for herbs, salad leaves, fungi and fruit to give the diner a true sense of place. Service is deliberately relaxed, informal and in the background so customers can feel welcomed and at home but looked after. This is reflected in attaining Good Food Guide readers Restaurant of the Year for Wales 2016. "We use locally sourced, ethical and traceable ingredients where practical and possible, to create a neighbourhood restaurant that locals can feel proud of," says Barnaby.

Sustainability is at the forefront of The Gallery's operations, dedicated to serving delicious and ethically sourced food. In 2016 it was awarded Welsh Food Made Good Champion by the Sustainable Restaurant Association for the third year running.

The Gallery in Barry has been named the Welsh Food Made Good Champion for the third year running. Recognised as the most sustainable restaurant in Wales - based on criteria such as ethical sourcing and the impact on society and the environment.

BRAISED OCTOPUS, BLOW TORCHED MACKEREL, CELERIAC & HOGWEED

SERVES 4

 Ancre Hill Estates, Pinot Noir, 2013 (Wales)

Ingredients

Braised Octopus

1 large octopus (beak removed)
1 tbsp olive oil
2 onions (diced)
2 carrots (diced)
4 sticks celery (diced)
4 cloves garlic (crushed)
1 bulb fennel (diced)
100g cooking chorizo (sliced)
3 bay leaves
2 tins chopped tomatoes
1 bottle red wine (full bodied)
3 tsp smoked paprika

Celeriac Purée

2 celeriac (peeled, diced)
200ml double cream
70g unsalted butter
white pepper (pinch of)

Mackerel

2 mackerel (filleted, pin-boned)
1 lemon (zest of)
½ orange (zest of)
50g flaked sea salt
20g caster sugar

Hogweed Oil

200g very fresh young shoots and leaves of hogweed (watercress can be used as an alternative)
40ml light olive oil
40ml rapeseed oil
20ml lemon juice
salt (pinch of)

Garnish

bronze fennel fronds

Method

For The Braised Octopus

Bring a large pan of unsalted water to a rolling boil. Boil the octopus for 2 minutes, then immediately remove and place into ice water. Allow to cool and repeat the process.

Heat the oil in a heavy-based, large pan, then add in the onion, carrot, celery, garlic, fennel and chorizo over a medium heat. Soften with no colour. Add all the remaining ingredients, bring to a simmer, then add the octopus. Cover and leave on a gentle simmer until the octopus is very tender, usually 3 hours depending on size.

Chef's Tip

The leftover cooking *liquor* from the octopus makes an incredible fish stew. Just add pieces of the spare octopus, warm through and serve with crusty bread for a hearty supper.

For The Celeriac Purée

Cover the celeriac in lightly salted water, bring to the boil and cook until very tender.

Remove the celeriac and drain in a fine sieve, squeezing out extra moisture with the back of a wooden spoon. Meanwhile, warm through the remaining ingredients in a pan.

Add the warm celeriac to a food blender. Add the liquid a little at a time and blend until desired consistency is reached. Adjust seasoning to taste and pass through a fine sieve.

For The Mackerel

Combine all the ingredients, less the mackerel. Set aside.

For The Hogweed Oil

Bring a pan of salted water up to a rolling boil, add the hogweed and bring back to the boil. Cook for 2 minutes, remove the hogweed and plunge straight into ice water.

Add the oils, lemon juice and hogweed to a food blender. Blitz to a very fine *emulsion*, then pass through a clean cloth. Adjust seasoning to your preference. Set aside.

To Serve

Cut the octopus into portions. Depending on size, 1 tentacle will serve 2 as a starter. Heat under a grill. Meanwhile warm the purée through (a cream whipper can be used if a lighter consistency is required in your final dish). Place the mackerel on a heatproof oven tray, sprinkle the lemon salt onto the fish and, at the last minute, blow torch the mackerel until just cooked. Assemble the dish as pictured and garnish with bronze fennel fronds.

ROAST LAMB RUMP, GOAT'S CHEESE CROQUETTE, SALT BAKED KOHLRABI, PEA & SAMPHIRE

SERVES 4

 Bodegas LAN Crianza, Rioja, 2011
(Spain)

Ingredients

Lamb
4 lamb rumps (trimmed, seasoned)
1 tbsp olive oil
4 cloves garlic
4 sprigs rosemary
20g butter

Salt Baked Kohlrabi
500g sea salt
500g plain flour
1 tbsp rosemary (finely chopped)
cold water (to bind)
2 kohlrabi (topped, tailed, peeled)

Pea Purée
1 litre light chicken stock
500g peas (fresh or frozen)

Goat's Cheese Croquettes
500g floury potatoes (peeled, roughly chopped)
100g soft goat's cheese
50g unsalted butter
1 egg yolk, 2 eggs (beaten)
70g plain flour
120g panko breadcrumbs

To Serve
samphire (*blanched*, glossed in butter)
broad beans (*blanched*, glossed in butter)
crispy cavolo nero, red wine jus

Chef's Tip
Salt baking works for any large root vegetables such as celeriac, turnip and swede.

Method

For The Roast Lamb Rumps
Preheat the oven to 220°C.
Sear the rumps in a hot, ovenproof frying pan in a little oil until lightly browned. Add the remaining ingredients, glossing each rump with the butter. Transfer to the oven for 15 minutes (pink) or 30 minutes (cooked through). Cover loosely in tin foil and allow to rest in a warm place for at least 10 minutes.

For The Salt Baked Kohlrabi (Prepare ahead)
Using a food processor with a dough hook attachment, mix all the dry ingredients and add cold water until a thick dough is created. Remove and wrap tightly in cling film, then allow to rest in the fridge for at least 2 hours.
Preheat the oven to 200°C.
Roll out the pastry onto a floured surface to about 0.8 cm thickness. Wrap both kohlrabis so there are no air gaps. Bake on a baking tray for 45 minutes. Leave to cool in the pastry for 10 minutes, then remove the crust. Using an apple corer, portion into cylinders. Be careful not to do this right to the edge of kohlrabi (as it will be too salty after being in contact with the salt pastry).

For The Pea Purée
Bring the stock up to the boil in a large pan, add the peas and bring back to boil. Cook for 3 minutes, then remove and submerge into ice water. Retain the chicken stock and place the peas into a food processor. Add the chicken stock a little at a time while blending until the desired consistency is reached. Pass through a fine sieve and check the seasoning.

For The Goat's Cheese Croquettes
Boil the potatoes in salted water until just cooked. Drain the water and shake the pan to remove any extra moisture. Push the potatoes through a ricer or mash and, while still warm, combine with the goat's cheese, butter, egg yolk and mix well. Check the seasoning, chill in the fridge, then roll into little sausages. Use the remaining ingredients to *pane* the croquettes and set aside.

To Serve
Warm through the purée. Deep fry the croquettes (180°C) until golden brown and piping hot in the centre. Reheat the portioned kohlrabi in the oven with no seasoning. Carve the rested meat and assemble the dish. Serve with red wine jus and samphire.

STRAWBERRY CHEESECAKE

SERVES 6

 Two Hands Wines Brilliant Disguise Moscato, Barossa Valley, 2015 (Australia)

Ingredients

Cheesecake Base

90g butter, 60g ground almonds
60g caster sugar
60g Demerara sugar
60g plain flour

Cheesecake Mix

150ml double cream
4 leaves bronze gelatine (soaked in cold water)
600g mascarpone, 250g crème fraîche
80g icing sugar
2 vanilla pods (seeds of)
1 orange (zest and ½ juice of)
1 lemon (zest of)

Strawberry Purée

90g caster sugar
750g fresh strawberries (hulled, quartered)
1 lemon (juice of)

Strawberry Jelly Top

250g strawberry purée
50g caster sugar
150ml water
4 leaves gelatine (soaked in cold water)

Strawberry Sorbet

30ml water
10ml lemon juice
60g caster sugar
350g strawberry purée

Strawberry Tuile & Coulis

150g strawberry purée, 40g caster sugar

Macerated Strawberries

50g fresh strawberries (hulled, quartered)
½ vanilla pod (husk and seeds of)
50ml sweet wine or vermouth
10g caster sugar

Garnish

strawberry powder, red vein sorrel leaves

Method

For The Cheesecake Base (Prepare ahead)

Preheat the oven to 180ºC.

Combine all the ingredients, except 30g of the butter, in a food processor. Transfer to a baking tray and cook for 15 minutes until golden brown. Allow to cool, then return to the food processor. Blitz to breadcrumbs. Melt the remaining 30g of butter and add to the breadcrumbs.

Line a rectangular, deep sided oven dish with 2 layers of cling film and press the biscuit base into it. Set in the fridge for 2 hours.

For The Cheesecake Mix

Heat the double cream, take off the heat and whisk through the softened gelatine. Pass through a fine sieve and reserve.

Whisk together all the other ingredients in large bowl, then fold through the double cream and gelatine mix. Layer on top of the set biscuit base and return to the fridge. Allow to set for 2 hours.

> **Chef's Tip**
>
> We use crème fraîche for a lighter cheesecake but you could easily replace this with cream cheese instead for a richer cheesecake.

For The Strawberry Purée (For use in sorbet, tuile & coulis)

Combine the sugar and strawberries, mix well and leave for 30 minutes at room temperature. Transfer to a blender, add the lemon juice and blitz to a purée. Pass through a very fine sieve.

To Make The Strawberry Jelly Top

Heat all the ingredients, apart from the gelatine, stirring to ensure the sugar has dissolved. Whisk through the soft gelatine leaves, then allow to cool. Carefully pour over the set cheesecake and return to fridge for 1 hour for the jelly to set.

For The Strawberry Sorbet

Heat the water, lemon and sugar until dissolved. Reduce to a thick syrup, then allow to cool in the fridge. Fold through the purée, then churn in an ice cream machine. Freeze until needed.

For The Strawberry Tuile & Coulis

Heat the purée and sugar to 90ºC in a pan stirring continuously, ensuring the sugar has melted. Divide the mix in half.

Spread half the mix in a thin layer onto a silicone sheet using a palette knife. Place in a dehydrator or oven at 70ºC (fan) until crisp. When dried, break into shards.

To Make The Macerated Strawberries

Combine all the ingredients in a bowl and leave in a warm place for 20 minutes.

To Serve

Cut the finished cheesecake into rectangular portions and decorate the plate with all the elements. Garnish as pictured.

096
GROVE OF NARBERTH

Molleston, Narberth, Pembrokeshire, SA67 8BX

01834 860 915
www.thegrove-narberth.co.uk Twitter: @GroveNarberth

Nestled in the heart of the beautiful Pembrokeshire countryside, the Grove is one of Wales' finest restaurants and a leading, small, luxury hotel. It is set within beautifully manicured lawns, flower borders, meadows and mature trees - and a region that offers a great selection of delicious ingredients. The Grove is today renowned as one of the country's most unique, privately owned venues.

The Grove's food has won national awards and critical acclaim, including 3 AA Rosettes, Wales Tourism Award for Best Place to Eat in Wales in 2011 and a cooking score of 6 in the Good Food Guide 2017.

The restaurant serves modern British food with global influences using the freshest, locally sourced ingredients, cooked by the executive chef Allister Barsby and his team. Much of the produce is grown in the Grove's extensive kitchen garden.

The Grove offers a truly intimate dining experience with warming log fires throughout the house. The restaurant is surrounded by trees, gardens and wildflower meadows to provide a magnificent setting whatever the time of year.

The terrace is also perfect for enjoying al fresco eating throughout the summer months.

Apart from the food, the Grove offers 26 intimate guest rooms and suites, the interiors individually designed to the highest standards.

Gaze out of the windows for scenic views of the Preseli mountains, or make the short trip to the Pembrokeshire National Park for stunning country walks.

The Grove of Narberth offers great food, fine wines and a wee bit of luxury in the most stunning part of Wales.

WARM QUAIL SALAD, CARAMELISED SHALLOTS, BRAISED CELERY, QUAIL TEA

SERVES 4

🍷 *Chorey-lès-Beaune, Domaine Maillard Père 2013, Burgundy (France)*

Ingredients

Quail

2 x 300g quails (legs removed from crown)
brine solution (90% water/10% salt, to cover)
duck fat (to cover), 50ml olive oil
50g unsalted butter, 2 cloves garlic, 4 sprigs thyme

Quail Tea

500g quail carcasses, 25ml vegetable oil
25g butter, 50g shallots (sliced)
200g button mushrooms (sliced)
25ml sherry vinegar, 100ml Madeira
750ml chicken stock, 750ml water
3 sprigs thyme, 1 bay leaf, 5g cumin seeds (toasted)
3g fennel seed (lightly toasted), ½ stick cinnamon
1 star anise, 1 strip dried orange zest
2g chicken bouillon powder, 25g chicken livers
50g egg whites, 50g ice, salt and pepper

Quail Sauce

350g quail carcasses (chopped small)
50ml vegetable oil, 25g butter, 50g shallots (sliced)
125g button mushrooms (sliced), 25ml port
100ml Madeira, 200ml veal glace
500ml chicken stock, 50ml double cream
10 black peppercorns, 1 bay leaf, 2 large sprigs thyme

Shallot Purée

500g shallots (sliced), 30g butter, 1 bay leaf
100ml chicken stock, 100ml water, salt and pepper

Braised Celery

3 sticks celery (peeled, cut into 2½cm diamonds)
25g unsalted butter, 30g onions (sliced)
1 clove garlic, 2 sprigs thyme, 1 bay leaf
100ml chicken stock, 200ml water, salt (pinch of)

Caramelised Shallots

10 small round shallots, 1 litre water, 20g salt
20ml blended olive oil, 30ml balsamic vinegar

Garnish

red chicory, pennywort leaves, Granny Smith apple
deep-fried celery leaves (drizzled with vinaigrette)

Method

For The Quail (Prepare ahead)

Submerge the legs in brine for 5 hours. Rinse and pat dry.
Confit the legs in duck fat in a small saucepan for 1 hour.
Remove from the fat and chill. Remove the thigh bones.
Preheat the oven to 185°C (fan).

Colour the crowns in oil and butter. Turn over, add the garlic and thyme and place in the oven for 5 minutes. Baste, remove the crowns and add the legs. Colour until crispy. Remove the breast from the crowns.

For The Quail Tea

Roast the carcasses in oil over a high heat, add the butter and roast for 2 minutes. Add the shallots with 125g of mushrooms and colour.

Add the vinegar and reduce to nothing. Stir in the Madeira and reduce by half. Add the stock, water, herbs, 1g fennel seeds, remaining spices, bouillon and a pinch of salt. Bring to the boil, skim and simmer for 45 minutes. Strain through a fine sieve. Leave to cool.

Blend the livers and egg whites. Whisk together with the remaining mushrooms and fennel seeds, ice and salt. Bring the stock to the boil and quickly whisk in the egg white mixture and, using a wooden spoon, stir back to the boil. Cook over a low heat for 20 minutes. Set aside for 10 minutes. Pass through muslin and season.

For The Quail Sauce

Colour the carcasses in hot oil, then add the butter. Stir in the shallots and mushrooms and sweat for 2 minutes. Add the port and Madeira and reduce by half. Stir in the remaining ingredients, bring to the boil and simmer for 30 minutes. Pass through a fine sieve. Reduce to desired consistency.

For The Shallot Purée

Sweat the shallots in butter and a pinch of salt for 10 minutes. Add the remaining ingredients, cover with greaseproof paper and simmer for 30 minutes. Blend for 5 minutes until smooth. Pass through a fine sieve.

For The Braised Celery

Heat the ingredients until the celery is tender.

For The Caramelised Shallots

Blanch the shallots for 5 minutes, then refresh in ice water and peel, leaving the root on. Cut in half lengthways. Fry, flat-side down in oil, in a hot, non-stick frying pan until dark. Season well. Remove from the heat and add the vinegar. Set aside.

To Serve

Ensure all elements are warm and garnish as pictured.

LINE CAUGHT COD, BLACK GARLIC, CROSNES, SAMPHIRE, BROWN SHRIMPS, LEMON VERBENA SCENTED JUS

SERVES 4

🍷 *Colheita Seleccionada, Adega de Pegões 2013, Peninsula de Setúbal (Portugal)*

Ingredients

Cod
650g cod loin (skinless)
25g table salt, 20ml olive oil
50g unsalted butter
lemon juice (spritz of)

Black Garlic Purée
200g black garlic
5ml balsamic vinegar
75ml Madeira
100ml water, 10g butter

Lemon Verbena Jus
1 turkey leg (chopped into large dice)
100ml vegetable oil
2 small onions (cut into rounds)
1 garlic head (cut in half)
5 sprigs thyme
5 sprigs lemon verbena
500ml water, 500ml chicken stock

Braised Crosnes
150g crosnes, 150ml water
150ml chicken stock
1 bay leaf, 2 sprigs thyme
butter (knob of), salt and pepper (pinch of)

Rosemary Oil
100ml blended olive oil, 10g rosemary (picked)

Rosemary Beurre Noisette
100g unsalted butter
20g rosemary, 10ml lemon juice

Garnish
150g samphire, 8 lemon segments
100g brown shrimps
50g hazelnuts (toasted, chopped)
10g chives (chopped), 8 sprigs sea rosemary

Method

For The Cod (Prepare ahead)
Sprinkle the cod with salt, cover and refrigerate for 5 hours. Rinse well, pat dry and cut into 4 portions.

Preheat the oven to 185°C (fan).

Heat a non-stick pan until smoking. Add the oil, then the cod. Colour for 1 minute, add the butter and place into the oven for 3 minutes. Turn the fish and return for 2 more minutes. Remove from the oven, squeeze some lemon juice over, baste and leave to rest for 2 minutes.

> **Chef's Tip**
> Be sure to use line caught cod from a reputable supplier. Quality fish really does speak for itself.

For The Black Garlic Purée
Bring all of the ingredients to the boil, then simmer for 20 minutes. Blend until smooth, season and pass through a fine sieve.

For The Lemon Verbena Jus
Preheat the oven to 180°C (fan).

Roast the turkey in the oil for 40 minutes until golden.

Remove from the oven and, on top of the stove, add the onions and garlic. Add the thyme, 3 sprigs of lemon verbena and *deglaze* with the water and chicken stock. Bring to the boil and reduce to a simmer. Skim any scum and cook for 3 hours. Pass through a fine sieve and reduce consistency. Add the remaining lemon verbena and set aside to infuse for 10 minutes.

For The Braised Crosnes
Bring all the ingredients to the boil, simmer for 20 minutes until tender, then allow to cool. To serve, drain the crosnes, then roast in a frying pan in a little butter.

For The Rosemary Oil
Heat the oil and rosemary to 80°C. Transfer to a blender and blend for 4 minutes. Pass through muslin cloth.

For The Rosemary Beurre Noisette
Melt the butter in a saucepan, then turn up the heat and cook to a nut brown colour. Add the rosemary and lemon juice. Set aside to infuse for 10 minutes. Pass through a fine sieve.

To Serve
Warm the shrimps, hazelnuts and chives in a little of the *beurre noisette*. Plate as pictured.

CHOCOLATE TART, CARAMELISED BANANA, POPCORN ICE CREAM, CARAMEL

SERVES 8

Botrytis Semillon, Barossa Valley, Peter Lehmann 2011 (Australia)

Ingredients

Chocolate Pastry
250g plain flour, 13g cocoa powder
2½g salt, 200g butter (diced)
100g icing sugar, 2 egg yolks
25g dark chocolate (melted)

70% Chocolate Ganache
200g 70% dark chocolate (chopped small)
14g butter
200ml double cream
14g trimoline, 12g glucose syrup

Popcorn Ice Cream
500ml whole milk
200ml double cream
25g milk powder
5 egg yolks, 75g sugar
2½g sea salt
40g freshly popped popcorn

Caramel Sauce
300g sugar, 50g glucose syrup
100ml water
300ml double cream
50g butter

Caramel Springs & Popcorn
150g sugar, 50g glucose syrup
50ml water
32 nicely shaped pieces popcorn

Chocolate Soil
300g sugar, 75ml water
120g dark chocolate (finely chopped)
60g white chocolate
20g cocoa powder
40ml extra virgin olive oil

Garnish
2 bananas (cut into diamond shapes, flat side dipped in sugar, caramelised with a blow torch)

23cm square, loose-bottomed tart case

Method

For The Chocolate Pastry
Sift the flour, cocoa powder and salt into a bowl and rub in the butter to a fine crumb. Add the icing sugar, yolks and chocolate. Refrigerate for 2 hours, remove and leave to rest for 30 minutes. Roll the pastry between 2 sheets of parchment until 2mm thick, trim to the size of the case and rest in the fridge for 30 minutes.
Preheat the oven to 160°C (fan).
Remove the parchment, lay flat onto the tart case base and blind bake for 20 minutes. Once cool, return the base to the tart case.

For The Chocolate Ganache
Place the chocolate and butter into a bowl. Bring the cream, trimoline and glucose to the boil and pour over the chocolate and butter, stirring constantly until amalgamated, thick and glossy. Pour into the tart case and leave to set in a cool place (not fridge) for 4 hours.

To Make The Popcorn Ice Cream
Bring the milk, cream and milk powder to the boil.
Whisk the egg yolks, sugar and salt together, then pour the cream over while still whisking. Place it back over a medium heat and while stirring, heat to 85°C. Pour into a blender, add the popcorn and blend until smooth. Pass through a fine sieve. Churn in an ice cream machine. Freeze for 1 hour.

For The Caramel Sauce
Place the sugar, glucose and water into a heavy-based pan and bring to the boil on a medium heat. Increase the heat and take it to a dark caramel. Carefully whisk in the cream, then the butter. Cool to room temperature. Store in a squeezy bottle.

For The Caramel Springs & Popcorn
Take the sugar, syrup and water to a blond caramel in a heavy-based pan over a high heat. Allow to cool.
Working quickly, wind the caramel around a knife steel. Heat the caramel further to loosen if it's too stiff.
Heat the caramel further, then carefully stir in the popcorn. Remove using tongs and cool, spaced out on parchment.

To Make The Chocolate Soil
Bring the sugar and water to 135°C over a high heat. Vigorously whisk in the dark chocolate. Leave to cool.
Preheat the oven to 160°C (fan).
Place the white chocolate onto a non-stick mat on a baking tray. Bake for 7-8 minutes to a dark caramel colour.
Pulse all the ingredients in a processor until it resembles soil.

To Serve
Plate as pictured.

106
THE HAND
AT LLANARMON

Llanarmon DC, Ceiriog Valley, Llangollen, LL20 7LD

01691 600 666
www.thehandhotel.co.uk Twitter: @thehandhotel

While The Hand at Llanarmon may be off the beaten track, set deep in the exquisite scenery of the Ceiriog valley, it is more than worth the visit. In 2014 Jonathan and Jackie Greatorex, (who had fallen in love with The Hand many years previously) acquired this wonderful inn. They have since lovingly refurbished all 13 bedrooms and more recently the Dining Room, where guests can enjoy spectacular cuisine. Food at The Hand has rightly received endless accolades and admiration for its consistent quality and innovation.

All dishes are freshly prepared on the premises and, as you would expect, the menu changes daily. You will find tempting starters such as Goat's Cheese Panna Cotta, or a perfect Parfait of Chicken Livers. Diners are further spoilt by excellent main course choices. Sublimely executed fish is often available; Chargrilled Monkfish, or perhaps Pan Fried Sea Bass. Carnivores rejoice at the Welsh Rib Eye Steak, or maybe a Sauté Fillet of Pork or Roast Rump of Welsh Lamb, accompanied by the freshest of vegetables.

Customers also appreciate The Hand's commitment to classics such as the Wagyu beef burger or melt-in-the-mouth pies. Vegetarian options are certainly not an afterthought, always delicious and never run-of-the-mill. However, do leave room for dessert, it would be a shame to forego Caramel Poached Pear with Cider, or a Valrhona Dark Chocolate Delice.

The Hand has built a strong reputation for superb cuisine over the years. Headed up by award-winning head chef Grant Mulholland and his dynamic team, diners can expect traditional yet inventive dishes in tranquil surroundings.

SCALLOP CEVICHE WITH CIDER POACHED PEAR, PICKLED RADISH & PISTACHIO NUTS

SERVES 4

Forge Cellars Finger Lakes Riesling 2013 (USA)

Ingredients

Scallops

4 large king scallops
salt (pinch of)
lemon juice (spritz of)

Poached Pear

1 hard conference pear (200g)
280ml cider
50g sugar

Pickled Radish

25ml white wine
25ml white wine vinegar
lemon juice (spritz of)
salt (pinch of)
25g sugar
200g radishes

Garnish

200g pistachio nuts (peeled)
micro herbs

Method

For The Scallops

Place 2 pieces of cling film on a flat surface. Lay the king scallops neatly in a line on the cling film.

Secure the edges of the cling film and lay the scallops flat in the freezer for 10-20 minutes. This will make it easier to slice them thinner.

For The Poached Pear

Peel the pear and dice into equal size pieces. Poach gently in the cider and sugar until just soft. Leave aside to cool.

For The Pickled Radish

Make the pickling *liquor* by heating the white wine, vinegar, lemon juice, salt and sugar in a pan until the sugar dissolves. Place in a plastic tub and store in the fridge to cool. Once cool, thinly slice the radishes and place in the *liquor* for at least an hour.

To Serve & Assemble

Slice the frozen scallops very thinly and arrange on a plate. Season with a pinch of salt and a little lemon juice.

Arrange the pickled radish on top of the scallop slices with a few peeled pistachios. Finish the dish with the poached pear and a few micro herbs.

Chef's Tip

Soaking the pistachio nuts in warm water for a couple of minutes makes them easier to peel.

POWIS CASTLE VENISON LOIN, CHARGRILLED BROCCOLI STALK, WATERCRESS PUREE, CRISPY QUAIL'S EGG

SERVES 4

 Super Nanny Goat Pinot Noir, Central Otago 2014 (New Zealand)

Ingredients

Venison

50g butter
1 garlic clove (crushed)
4 sprigs thyme
500g venison loin

Venison Sauce

butter (knob of)
500g venison bones
50g carrot (chopped)
50g onion (chopped)
1 bay leaf
2 sprigs thyme
1 litre good quality veal or beef stock
50ml cassis liqueur

Watercress Purée

400g watercress
70g butter
30ml water
salt (pinch of)
ice cubes (handful of)

Chargrilled Broccoli Stalk

4 large stalks broccoli (peeled, trimmed)
salt and pepper
olive oil (drizzle of)

Crispy Quail's Eggs

oil (drizzle of)
8 quail's eggs
salt and pepper

Garnish

micro coriander

Method

For The Venison

Heat a frying pan over a medium heat.

Add the butter and, when foaming, add the garlic, thyme and venison loin. *Sauté* for about 8-10 minutes, turning occasionally until brown all over. Remove from the pan and set aside. Keep warm until ready to serve.

> **Chef's Tip**
>
> When resting the venison, keep the juices from the meat and add them to the sauce.

For The Venison Sauce

Heat a *sauté* pan. Add the butter and venison bones and cook until golden brown. Stir in the carrots, onions, bay leaf, thyme and stock and reduce by half.

Strain the bones and vegetables and spoon off any excess fat. Reduce the liquid to your desired consistency and finish with cassis.

For The Watercress Purée

Pick the watercress leaves from the stalks.

Place a suitable sized pan on the stove, heat then add the butter, water and watercress to the hot pan. Add a pinch of salt and cook for just 2 minutes. When the watercress is cooked, add the ice.

Drain and transfer to a blender. Blitz until smooth.

For The Chargrilled Broccoli Stalk

Preheat the oven to 180ºC.

Slice the broccoli stalks into 2cm lengths. Place onto a very hot chargrill pan to achieve the chargrill marks.

Season with salt and pepper and a touch of olive oil, then transfer to the oven for around 5 minutes.

For The Crispy Quail's Eggs

Heat a non-stick pan with a little oil until hot but not smoking. Gently crack the eggs into the pan and cook for 1-1½ minutes until slightly crispy at the edges. Season with salt and pepper.

To Serve

Spoon the watercress purée onto the plates. Carve the venison loin and arrange on top of the purée, adding the broccoli and eggs as pictured. Garnish with micro coriander and serve with the venison sauce.

EARL GREY ICED PARFAIT WITH RUM BABA, RASPBERRIES & DEEP FRIED MINT LEAVES

SERVES 4

 Domaine de Grange, Neuve Monbazillac 2011
(France)

Ingredients

Earl Grey Iced Parfait

20g Earl Grey tea leaves
300ml warm water
100ml whole milk
80g egg yolks
150g caster sugar
5g gelatine (soaked in cold water)
250ml whipped cream
25ml dark rum

Rum Baba

3 medium eggs
12g honey
5g dried yeast
salt (pinch of)
125g plain flour
75g butter (melted, at room temperature)

Rum Syrup

200g caster sugar
200ml water
50ml dark rum
1 orange (zest of)
1 lemon (zest of)
1 vanilla pod (halved)

Crispy Mint

2 sprigs mint
icing sugar (to dust)

Garnish

1 punnet raspberries
4 ramekins or dariole moulds
4 mini savarin moulds

Method

For The Earl Grey Iced Parfait (Prepare ahead)

Infuse the tea in warm water, strain and add the milk.

Whisk the egg yolks with the sugar over a *bain-marie* and cook to 84°C. Stir in the gelatine and chill. When chilled but not yet set, fold in the whipped cream and rum. Spoon the mixture into the ramekins or dariole moulds and freeze.

For The Rum Babas

Mix the eggs, honey, yeast and salt in a large mixing bowl. Gradually sift in the flour to create a smooth batter. Slowly pour the melted butter into the batter mix and stir well.

Divide the batter into the savarin moulds until half full.
Leave at room temperature to double in size, reaching the top of the moulds.

Preheat the oven to 180°C.

Bake the babas for 8-10 minutes until firm to the touch and golden brown. Remove from the moulds and leave to cool.

For The Rum Syrup

Bring all the ingredients to the boil in a saucepan, then reduce to a simmer. Soak each baba in the syrup for no longer than 20 seconds, then place on a wire rack to cool.

For The Crispy Mint

Wash and pat dry the large mint leaves. Deep fry until crispy, then dust with icing sugar.

To Serve

Place the soaked rum baba in the centre of a large plate. Remove the iced parfait from the moulds and sit next to the baba. Garnish with raspberries and crispy mint leaves.

> **Chef's Tip**
>
> Remove the parfait from the freezer a couple of minutes before serving to allow it to soften. The parfait can be frozen in one large container and scooped into a ball for serving if you don't have ramekins or dariole moulds.

THE HARDWICK

Old Raglan Road, Abergavenny, NP7 9AA

01873 854 220
www.thehardwick.co.uk Twitter: @the_hardwick

The Hardwick was created by multi-award-winning chef Stephen Terry. He wasn't looking for glory when he opened it - though glory came and found him. Consistently ranked among the best in the UK, The Hardwick is a warm and welcoming restaurant with rooms that serve seasonal food at its best.

Chef Terry changes his menu according to the produce available. He has strong connections with local artisans, making sure the best flavours of Wales are always available.

Terry learned his craft under Marco Pierre White and alongside Gordon Ramsay before striking out on his own. He won 2 Michelin stars at two separate venues, including one for The Walnut Tree, located just down the road from The Hardwick.

And then began his labour of love. The Hardwick was a local pub when Terry bought it with his wife Jo, and they transformed it, creating a must-visit, destination restaurant with contemporary rooms for guests. It has been expanded considerably, creating an award-winning blend of trend and tradition.

"We're not trying to reinvent the wheel," says Terry. "We're just trying to respect the beautiful ingredients that come to the kitchen door. The word we hear most from our guests is this: 'tasty'. And if all of our dishes are tasty, we can live with that."

Tasty dishes from a winning team, The Hardwick has found a recipe for success.

The Hardwick doesn't have a trophy cabinet, though it should have. It consistently ranks among the UK's best and chef Stephen Terry is a serial award-winner. His delicious food wows judges, critics and customers alike.

the HARDWICK

TOMATOES ON TOAST

SERVES 4

Fiano, Luigi Maffini, 2014
(Italy)

Ingredients

½ red onion (peeled, cut into wedges)
2 little gem lettuces (halved)
4 quality, large Heritage tomatoes (thinly sliced)
4 tbsp extra virgin olive oil
1 tbsp red wine vinegar
2 salted anchovy fillets (finely chopped)
½ small chilli (finely chopped)
1 small clove garlic (finely chopped)
sea salt (pinch of)
4 slices grilled sourdough
1 handful broad beans (cooked, podded)

Method

To Make & Assemble The Dish

Chargrill the onion and little gem lettuce halves. Separate the onion layers and set aside.

Marinate the tomatoes in the olive oil and vinegar with the anchovies, chilli, garlic and a little sea salt for 5 minutes.

Meanwhile, grill the slices of sourdough, then place an even amount of tomatoes on each slice of bread.

Toss the broad beans and little gem lettuce halves in the same bowl and place on the plate. Dress the chargrilled onion pieces with a little olive oil and sea salt. Arrange on the plates and serve.

Chef's Tip

Invest in the best quality bread and tomatoes.

CHARGRILLED PEPPER, MOZZARELLA & PESTO

SERVES 4

🍷 *Radikon Ribolla Gialla, Friuli-Venezia, Giulia, 2008 (Italy) or any Italian orange wine*

Method

To Prepare

Chargrill the peppers, then peel them, remove the seeds and cut the flesh into 4. Lightly chargrill the radicchio lettuce leaves.

Slice each mozzarella ball into 4.

Finely slice the shallot and deep fry until crispy.

> **Chef's Tip**
>
> With the peppers, you could put them under the grill or a blow torch is always good!

For The Pickled Kohlrabi

Bring the vinegar to the boil with the chilli, pour it over the kohlrabi and leave to pickle until the liquid has cooled.

To Plate

Layer the mozzarella and grilled pepper with pesto.

Dress the radicchio and radish with olive oil and lemon juice. Season with salt. Finish by garnishing the radicchio with the diced kohlrabi and fried shallots and serve as pictured.

Ingredients

2 large Italian yellow or red peppers
8 large leaves radicchio lettuce
4 x 100g balls buffalo mozzarella
1 shallot (peeled)
4 tbsp good quality pesto
12 radishes (finely sliced)
2 tbsp extra virgin olive oil
lemon juice (spritz of)
sea salt (to taste)

Pickled Kohlrabi

vinegar (to cover)
1 chilli (halved)
1 small kohlrabi (peeled, diced)

VANILLA PANNA COTTA, STRAWBERRY, TOMATO, BASIL & POLENTA CRUMB

SERVES 4

🍷 *Recioto Soave 'La Broia' Roccolo Grassi, Vento, 2008 (Italy)*

Ingredients

Vanilla Panna Cotta

285ml whole milk
568ml double cream
60g caster sugar
1 vanilla pod (scraped)
2 leaves gelatine (soaked in cold water)

Basil Syrup

50g caster sugar
50ml water
1 small bunch basil (picked)

Polenta Crumb

90g polenta
40g plain white flour
45g caster sugar
40g butter

Garnish

20 strawberries
2 ripe tomatoes

Method

For The Vanilla Panna Cotta

Boil the milk and cream, add the sugar and vanilla pod and seeds, then stir in the gelatine until dissolved. Pass through a fine sieve and allow to cool. As the panna cotta thickens and sets, pour equal amounts between 4 serving plates. Allow to finish setting in the fridge for 3-4 hours.

> **Chef's Tip**
>
> Before pouring the panna cotta onto the plate, it looks better if you allow the mixture to start setting so that the vanilla is suspended.

For The Basil Syrup

Boil the sugar and water to make a simple syrup. Leave to cool to 37°C, then add the basil and blitz. Pass through a fine sieve.

For The Polenta Crumb

Preheat the oven to 150°C (fan).

Combine all the ingredients together to a crumb consistency and bake for 20 minutes. Allow to cool.

To Plate

Dress the panna cottas as pictured, or how you so desire.

126
HARE & HOUNDS

Aberthin, Cowbridge, Vale of Glamorgan, CF71 7LG

01446 774 892
www.hareandhoundsaberthin.com Twitter: @Hare__Hounds

A transformed local pub, the Hare & Hounds was taken over in 2015 by Tom and Sarah Watts-Jones and Alex Howells. Head chef Tom has returned to his home village after training in kitchens in London at the Anchor & Hope and the Michelin starred St John.

The restaurant offers a small, daily changing, seasonal menu. The kitchen prides itself on using the very best local produce, along with their own kitchen garden and smallholding to dictate what is on the menu each day. Everything served is made from scratch on the premises, from sourdough and focaccia breads and home-cultured butter, to charcuterie and fresh pasta. The chefs do all of their own butchery, often using lesser known cuts of the animal in their nose-to-tail style of cooking.

The bar remains a thriving local watering hole, run by general manager Alex, with his vast knowledge on their fantastic range of craft beers, great lagers and fine wines. There is always a variety of seasonal homemade drinks on offer, including the signature Seasonal Prosecco Fizz.

The dining room itself is relaxed and welcoming with focus on the open kitchen. Alongside the à la carte menu, the kitchen also serves a nine course tasting menu, which gives a wonderful taste of everything on offer that day. This can be made even more special with wine matching.

Regular events are also popular, from bread-making evenings to tasting menus matched with drinks from beer to Champagne, often including a talk from the brewer or producer.

Awards, blogger and reviewer recognitions are all flooding in for this local restaurant, along with diners from far and wide. Now there are even plans in motion for boutique B&B rooms.

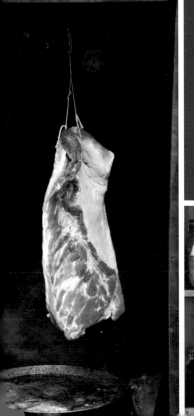

The Hare & Hounds serves excellent quality food and drink in relaxed and informal surroundings.

GRILLED RAZOR CLAMS, TOMATO, CHILLI & CUCUMBER

SERVES 4

 Picpoul de Pinet, Domaine de Belle Mare 2015, Languedoc (France)

Ingredients

Smoked Tomato Purée

200g cherry tomatoes (halved)
½ tsp smoked paprika
4 sprigs thyme
salt and pepper (to taste)

Tomato Concasse

3 plum tomatoes
1 large red chilli (seeds removed)
3 sprigs thyme
1 lemon (fine zest of)
175ml rapeseed oil
salt and pepper

Razor Clams

12 medium-sized razor clams
salt and pepper
lemon juice (spritz of)

To Garnish

¼ cucumber (finely chopped)
fresh dill (pinch of)

Method

For The Smoked Tomato Purée

Preheat the oven to 150°C.

Combine all the ingredients in a baking tray, mix thoroughly and bake for 1 hour until almost burnt. Purée in a blender and pass through a sieve. Set aside.

For The Tomato Concasse

Blanch the tomatoes in boiling water for 10-20 seconds, then refresh in ice water until cold. Peel, remove all seeds and finely dice. Place in a mixing bowl. Finely dice the chilli and thyme and add to the tomatoes. Add the finely grated zest of the lemon and the rapeseed oil and mix. Season to taste. Set to one side.

For The Razor Clams

Under a hot grill, heat the razor clams until they open (approximately 1-2 minutes). Once all have opened, remove the meat from the shell (keeping the shells to one side). Cut off the sand sack and discard. Chop the meat into ½cm chunks and place into a small pan with the tomato mixture. Cook over a low heat for approximately 2 minutes. Season to taste and add a squeeze of lemon.

To Serve

Arrange the clam and tomato concasse mixture in the shells and dot with the purée. Garnish with a sprinkle of finely diced cucumber and dill.

> **Chef's Tip**
>
> This is also delicious as a quick pasta dish. Instead of placing the mix back in the shells, add it to some fresh pappardelle.

ROAST TORGELLY FARM LAMB, PAN FRIED LAMB SWEETBREADS, PEA, BACON & MINT

SERVES 4

Rioja Reserva, Marqués de Riscal 2012
(Spain)

Ingredients

1 medium-sized lamb leg muscle

Lamb Sweetbreads & Sauce

100g Pembrokeshire potatoes (halved)
rapeseed oil (splash of)
500g lamb sweetbreads (cleaned)
200g smoked bacon lardons
red wine vinegar (splash of)
200ml lamb stock
75g butter
100g fresh peas
mint (small bunch of)
salt and pepper

To Garnish

pea shoots (handful of)
edible flowers such as nasturtiums or borage
(handful of)

Method

For The Lamb Leg Muscle

Preheat the oven to 220°C.

Roast the lamb leg to your desired colour - 6 minutes will give medium rare.

For The Lamb Sweetbreads & Sauce

Ensure that the sweetbreads are thoroughly cleaned before cooking.

Boil the potatoes until soft. Heat a heavy-based frying pan over a high heat with a splash of rapeseed oil and add the sweetbreads. When they start to colour, add the bacon. When there is a good colour on both, add in the potatoes and brown them slightly too. Add a splash of red wine vinegar, the lamb stock and butter and cook until reduced. Once the liquid has reduced, toss in the peas and fresh mint. Season as desired.

To Serve

Slice the lamb leg into equal sized portions. Add a spoonful or two of the sweetbreads to each plate, then top with the lamb leg and a sprinkling of pea shoots and edible flowers.

Chef's Tip

If you can, it's best to buy fresh sweetbreads rather than frozen. To save time you can always buy frozen peas..

PRALINE & ORANGE CHOCOLATE BAR

SERVES 8

Muscat de Saint Jean de Minervois, Domaine de Barroubio, Languedoc (France)

Ingredients

Praline Base

200g caster sugar
200ml water
400g mixed nuts (hazelnuts, almonds, walnuts)

Chocolate & Orange Filling

200g dark cooking chocolate
3 eggs (separated)
3 egg whites
125g sugar
150g toasted hazelnuts
1 orange (zest and juice of)

To Assemble

100g butter
garnish of your choice, eg honeycomb,
strawberries, hazelnuts

65mm gastronorm or 2½ litre dish
(lined with baking parchment)

Method

For The Praline Base

To make a caramel, heat the sugar and water in a pan on a high heat until golden. Spread the nuts on a baking tray and pour the caramel over the nuts. Leave to cool. Once cool, blitz in a blender until the nuts are a coarse consistency.

For The Chocolate & Orange Filling

Melt the chocolate in a glass bowl over a pan of boiling water. Once melted, stir in the egg yolks and leave to one side. Mix the 6 egg whites and sugar in a food mixer to stiff peaks. Fold the 2 mixtures gently together. Chop the hazelnuts finely and add to the mixture, along with the zest and juice of the orange.

To Assemble

Melt the butter and mix with the praline base. Pour this into the gastronorm or dish and place in the fridge for at least 10 minutes until firm. Pour the chocolate and orange filling onto the base and leave to set in the fridge for at least 2 hours.

To Serve

Remove the chocolate bar in the baking parchment from the dish. Heat a sharp knife under hot running water and slice the bar into the desired portion sizes. For the best finish, reheat the knife before cutting each portion. The portions can go back in the fridge if required.

When ready to serve, add the garnish of your choice.

> **Chef's Tip**
> This keeps in the fridge for up to a week, so can be made well in advance.

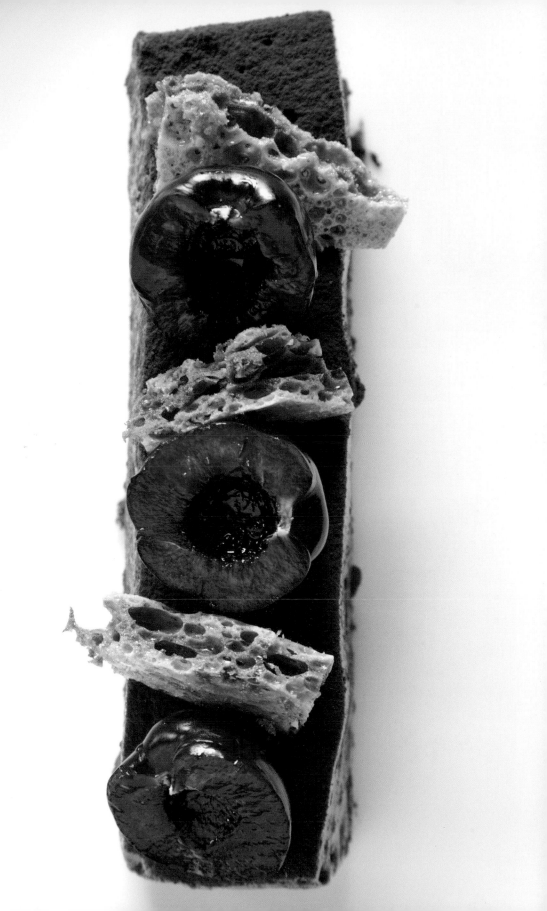

136
LLANSANTFFRAED COURT

Clytha, Llanvihangel Gobion, Nr Abergavenny, Monmouthshire, South Wales, NP7 9BA

01873 840 678
www.llch.co.uk Facebook: LLCHotel Twitter: @Llchotel

Llansantffraed Court is a 4 star, food-led, country house hotel, set in 20 acres of stunning parkland, in the foodie golden triangle of rural Monmouthshire, and on the edge of the Brecon Beacons National Park and the Wye Valley. The grand, stately exterior belies the unstuffy and warm nature of the welcome Mike Morgan and his team offer.

The huge, restored, Victorian walled vegetable garden, along with the area's passionate, artisan food suppliers drives the seasonality of the menus.

Expect a genuine, friendly 'Croeso', easy comfort and a focus on the very best, locally sourced food cooked to exacting, modern fine dining standards. The many years of Michelin starred experience in the kitchen brigade make the dining offer look deceptively simple, with accurate cooking, stunning presentation and clear flavours the backbone of a now highly regarded dining room at accessible prices.

The beamed 17th Century dining room, decorated in a muted, classic modern style with quality table linen and high end glassware, is the perfect backdrop for the food. Together with comfortable lounges, open fires, a south facing sunny terrace overlooking the lake, and a carefully chosen 200 bin wine list, with all wines available by the glass, makes it a perfect place for a short break.

Llansantffraed has a hard earned reputation for high standard food, with accolades such as 2 AA Rosettes for 20 consecutive years, listings in the Michelin Guide for the same period, shortlisted for AA Wine List of the Year for the last 11 years and winner of Best Small Restaurant in the National Tourism Awards in 2013 - recognition that is commensurate with the passion shown in every plate and glass.

"Seasonality runs through everything we do here. The fabulous walled kitchen garden is the DNA for some accomplished cooking by Tim McDougall and his dedicated brigade. Food yards, not food miles." - Mike Morgan, owner & director.

POACHED CARDIGAN BAY MACKEREL, SALAD OF LLANSANTFFRAED GARDEN POTATOES, WHIPPED OLIVE OIL

SERVES 4

 Biecher & Schaal Grand Cru Riesling, Sommerberg, Alsace 2012 (France)

Ingredients

Mackerel

20g fresh dill
20g lemon (zest of, finely chopped)
20g table salt
20g caster sugar
4 mackerel fillets (very fresh, pin bones removed)
vegetable, light olive or rapeseed oil (to poach)

Potato Salad

200g salad potatoes (peeled)
vinaigrette (to dress)
salt and pepper

Whipped Olive Oil

60ml extra virgin olive oil
3ml white balsamic vinegar
salt (pinch of)
sugar (pinch of)
100ml boiling water
½g xanthan gum
1 leaf bronze gelatine (soaked in cold water)

Honey & Mustard Dressing

15g honey
30g crème fraîche
30g Dijon mustard
salt, pepper and sherry vinegar (to taste)

To Serve

crème fraîche
freshly ground black pepper
lemon juice (spritz of)
dill leaves, baby salad, cucumber

Method

For The Mackerel

Finely chop the dill stalks and leaves. Reserve some nice leaves for garnish. Combine the dill, zest, salt and sugar and lightly coat the fillets on both sides with the mixture. Refrigerate for 1 hour, then wash off the cure mixture by dipping the fillets in a bowl of cold water. Do not run under the tap as this may break up the fish. Dry the fillets and keep in the fridge until ready to cook.

For The Potato Salad

Cut the potatoes into even-sized pieces. Place in a pan of cold water, add a little salt and bring to a simmer. When just cooked, strain the potatoes and immediately dress with vinaigrette. Add salt and pepper to taste. Keep at room temperature.

> **Chef's Tip**
> If you don't have home grown salad potatoes, try to find Charlotte or Ratte potatoes as a substitute. We use an apple corer to make cylinders and a small Parisienne cutter to make little balls, but simple potato slices or cubes will work just as well.

For The Whipped Olive Oil

Start to whisk the oil, vinegar, salt and sugar, ideally in an electric bowl mixer, while the water comes to the boil. Add the xanthan gum to the mixing bowl, then squeeze the gelatine leaf dry and drop it into the pan, immediately pouring the just boiled water onto the oil mixture while whisking continuously. Whisk until the oil is cold and frothy. For an even lighter result, place the whipped oil into a cream whipper, charge with 1 gas charge and release the whole batch into a bowl. Keep at room temperature.

For The Honey & Mustard Dressing

Mix the honey, crème fraîche and mustard together, then add salt, pepper and sherry vinegar to taste.

To Assemble The Dish

Warm enough oil to cover the mackerel fillets in a sauté pan. Poach the fish at 48°C for 12 minutes. Alternatively, place the fillets in an ovenproof dish and heat the oil in a pan to about 65°C (until too hot for your finger) and pour over the fish. The skin will peel easily from the fish when it is cooked. Arrange the potato salad on 4 serving plates, dot with mustard dressing, whipped oil, and dots of crème fraîche for extra richness. Flake the mackerel fillets, reserving 1 small piece with the skin on for each plate. Season with fresh black pepper and lemon juice. Garnish as pictured.

FILLET OF BRECON BEEF, BRAISED SHORT RIB, SPRING ONION EMULSION, LOVAGE, GREENS

SERVES 4

 Villa Belvedere, Valpolicella Classico Superiore, Ripasso, Veneto, 2012 (Italy)

Ingredients

Braised Short Rib & Jus

2 Welsh beef short ribs (on the bone)
1 tbsp olive oil
1 carrot, 1 onion, 1 stick celery, 1 clove garlic
(roughly chopped)
10g tomato purée
10g plain flour
125ml red wine
1 bay leaf
1 sprig thyme
500ml homemade beef or chicken stock
20g bone marrow (optional)

Spring Onion Emulsion

1 bunch spring onions
500ml light olive or pomace oil (heated to 70°C)
parsley (handful of, optional)
500ml homemade chicken stock

Lovage Purée

150ml double cream
80g lovage leaves
salt and pepper

Beef Fillet

olive oil
400g piece of Brecon beef fillet (well aged)
butter (knob of)

To Serve

fresh beans
chard leaf
potato purée
sautéed mushrooms
4 spring onions (*blanched*, glazed in butter)

Method

For The Short Rib & Jus

Preheat the oven to 150°C.

Brown the ribs in a little oil. Remove the meat and add the vegetables. As they colour, reduce the heat and thoroughly stir in the purée, then the flour and herbs. *Deglaze* the pan with the wine and reduce until it coats the vegetables. Return the ribs to the pan, add the stock and bring to a simmer. Cover and roast for 2-3 hours, adding more water if necessary, until the meat falls from the bone. Remove the meat from the pan and set aside to cool. Pass the *liquor* through a sieve and reduce, adding a little bone marrow to deepen the flavour if desired.

For The Spring Onion Emulsion

Thinly slice the green of the onions and place in a heatproof liquidiser. Pour the hot oil in and blitz. Add parsley for extra colour. Pass the oil through a sieve into a jug and allow to settle. Pour off the green oil which rises to the surface. Discard the watery liquid beneath.

Slice the white part of the onions and place in a pan with the stock. Reduce to 100ml. Pass this into a bowl then, using an electric whisk, start to *emulsify* the oil and stock together. Start very slowly, a drop of oil at a time, then speed up a little as it thickens to a mayonnaise consistency.

For The Lovage Purée

Boil the cream, add the lovage and cook until soft. Liquidise and, if necessary, return to the pan to thicken. Season.

Chef's Tip

If you don't have lovage, use celery leaves and parsley. A drop of Welsh ale in the jus will also add a nice, herby bitterness.

To Cook The Beef

Season the fillet and brown in a little oil in a skillet. Remove the short rib meat from the bone. Portion and brown on one side in the same pan as the fillet. When the fillet is nicely coloured, turn down the heat and add a knob of butter. Baste the meats until the butter has almost stopped foaming. Remove from the pan and rest for 10 minutes. Serve the fillet rare!

To Serve

Arrange the vegetables on the plate with a piece of rib and a thick slice of fillet for each diner. Dot the lovage and spring onion *emulsion* around the plate and finish with a glazed spring onion.

LLANSANTFFRAED GARDEN RHUBARB, VANILLA PANNA COTTA

SERVES 4

🍷 *Ancre Hill Estates, Sparkling Rosé, Monmouthshire, 2010 (Wales)*

Ingredients

Vanilla Panna Cotta

1 fresh vanilla pod (scraped)
450ml whole milk
50ml double cream
100g caster sugar
2 bronze gelatine leaves (soaked in cold water)

Rhubarb Jus

2kg pink rhubarb stalks
660g caster sugar

Rhubarb Sorbet

500ml rhubarb jus
50g trimolene (invert sugar syrup)

Rhubarb Gel

500ml rhubarb jus
5g gellan gum type F

To Serve

almonds (crushed)
rhubarb pieces (poached in Sauternes)

4 pastry or dariole moulds/glasses/ramekins

Method

For The Vanilla Panna Cotta

Bring the vanilla seeds and pod, milk, cream and sugar to the boil, then remove from the heat.

Leave to infuse for 5 minutes, then dissolve the gelatine in the panna cotta mix. Stir well and pass through a sieve into a jug. Pour into suitable moulds. To avoid the vanilla seeds sinking to the bottom of the moulds, stir once when the panna cottas have cooled but are not yet set. Refrigerate for 3 hours or until set.

For The Rhubarb Jus

Slice the rhubarb fairly thinly and place in a large mixing bowl. Add the sugar and mix to coat the rhubarb. Tightly cling film the top of the bowl, then place it on top of a large pan of simmering water. A clear syrup will slowly start to appear. When all the rhubarb appears cooked, line a colander with a clean muslin cloth and place over a suitable container. Pass the syrup through the cloth and leave to cool.

> **Chef's Tip**
>
> For a simpler dish, make the rhubarb jus as instructed and use this as a pouring sauce rather than making the gel and the sorbet.

For The Rhubarb Sorbet

Mix the jus and the trimolene together and churn in an ice cream machine. Freeze until required.

For The Rhubarb Gel

Bring the jus to a gentle simmer and whisk in the gellan gum. Whisk for 1 minute at 90°C or above, then pour into a bowl set over ice water. Using a hand blender, pulse the gel as it sets to achieve a smooth texture. Transfer to a piping bag. If lumps form, simply liquidise the gel briefly once it is cold, then pass through a sieve.

To Assemble The Dish

If using a mould, dip in hot water to release the panna cottas, then turn out onto a plate. Pipe the rhubarb gel around the plate. Sit the sorbet on top of some crushed almonds to stop it moving. Garnish with pieces of rhubarb poached in Sauternes.

146
THE NEWBRIDGE ON USK

Newbridge on Usk, Tredunnock, Usk, NP15 1LY

01633 410 262
www.celtic-manor.com/newbridge-on-usk Twitter: @TheCelticManor

Occupying an idyllic location on the banks of the River Usk, this charming 200-year-old country inn with rooms is something of a secret hideaway.

The beautiful riverside setting can be enjoyed from a charming patio, making it perfect for al fresco dining in the summer, and inside, the rustic rooms with their wooden floorboards, comfy sofas, nooks and crannies all make for an exceptionally cosy rural retreat.

Now part of the Celtic Manor collection, the Newbridge on Usk serves lovingly cooked, modern British cuisine with a sophisticated touch from head chef Adam Whittle. Its emphasis on using local produce is amply demonstrated by the vegetables that are sourced from its own kitchen garden.

Adam served his apprenticeship at Celtic Manor before progressing his career at the Michelin starred Crown at Whitebrook and taking his first head chef position at the White Hart Village Inn in Llangybi, where he held 2 AA Rosettes. He has regained the same award of 2 AA Rosettes at the Newbridge and has also won the restaurant a listing in the Good Food Guide.

At weekends, diners can enjoy an afternoon of relaxed jazz and swing to accompany one of the best Sunday lunches in the Usk Valley, then work off their excesses exploring the surrounding countryside on one of many local walking trails. As well as lunch and dinner, The Newbridge on Usk serves an elegant cream tea overlooking the river.

The restaurant with rooms is also the perfect setting for a romantic gourmet escape, each of the six bedrooms being beautifully furnished with oak and teak pieces, roll top baths and storm showers.

The beautiful riverside setting can be enjoyed from a charming patio, making it perfect for al fresco dining in the summer, and inside, the rustic rooms with their wooden floorboards, comfy sofas, nooks and crannies all make for an exceptionally cosy rural retreat.

SOY & SESAME QUAIL, SPATZLE, CAVOLO, BURNT AUBERGINE & CORIANDER

SERVES 4

♟ *Poggio Argentiera Rosato, 2012*
(Italy)

Ingredients

Soy & Sesame Quail

100ml soy sauce
25ml sesame oil
25ml mirin (rice wine vinegar)
10ml honey
10ml sherry vinegar
4 quail (8 breast and leg halves)

Spätzle

200g plain flour
¾ tbsp semolina or rice flour
2 eggs
50ml sparkling water
50ml whole milk
salt

Burnt Aubergine Purée

250g aubergine
oil (to brush)
40g caster sugar
15g lemon juice
¼ clove garlic (finely grated)
5g thyme

Cavolo Nero

8 medium leaves cavolo nero (washed)
butter (knob of)
salt and pepper

Garnish

micro coriander

Method

For The Soy & Sesame Quail (Prepare ahead)

Combine the marinade ingredients and mix well. Place the quail halves into the marinade, cover and refrigerate for 24 hours.

Preheat the oven to 180°C (fan).

Pan fry the quail halves in a little oil over a high heat until sealed, then transfer to the oven for 3-6 minutes. Remove and rest.

> **Chef's Tip**
>
> Quail can be eaten pink (slightly underdone) which will help retain moistness, so be sure not to overcook.

For The Spätzle

Combine all the ingredients to form a batter, cover and leave to rest. Meanwhile, put a large pan of salted water on to boil. Once boiling, press the batter through a spätzle press or a large holed colander into the boiling water to form pasta like pieces. Simmer until the pieces float, then remove and set aside.

For The Burnt Aubergine Purée

Preheat the oven to 180°C (fan).

Slice the aubergine into 1cm thick slices lengthways, brush with oil and chargrill on both sides until heavily coloured. Place into an ovenproof dish and add all other ingredients. Cover tightly and bake for 20 minutes or until almost all of the liquid has evaporated. Remove from the oven and transfer to a blender. Blend until smooth. Check seasoning and keep warm.

To Assemble

Pan fry the spätzle pieces in a little oil or butter to slightly crisp the outside, then transfer to the plate. Lightly cook the cavolo nero in a knob of butter until just wilted, season. Dot the aubergine purée onto the plate and place the cavolo nero and quail on top. Garnish with micro coriander.

STONE BASS, MUSSELS, COURGETTE & ASPARAGUS

SERVES 4

🍷 *Les Trois Brises Sauvignon Gewürztraminer, 2015 (France)*

Ingredients

4 x 120g stone bass fillets (centre cut portions, seasoned)
1 tbsp oil

Mussels

24 mussels (cleaned)
250ml cider

Courgette Sauce

25g unsalted butter
4 courgettes
350ml semi-skimmed milk
reserved mussel cooking liquid (strained)
30g spinach
salt

To Serve

8 green asparagus spears (woody ends removed)
kale, spinach, chard (washed)
any one or a mix of the above
butter (knob of)
salt (pinch of)

Method

For The Mussels

Place a large pan over a high heat. Once hot, add the mussels and cider and cover. Shake to move the mussels around and remove from the heat once the mussels have opened (this should only take a couple of minutes). Sit a colander over a bowl and pour the mussels into it. Once cool enough to handle, remove the mussels from their shells. Discard the shells and any mussels that haven't opened. Set the mussels and liquid aside.

For The Courgette Sauce

Melt the butter in a medium pan over a medium to high heat.

Meanwhile, cut the courgettes into small chunks and add to the pan. Cook until starting to soften, then season, add the milk and mussel liquid and cook for a further 10 minutes. Add the spinach, stir and remove from the heat. Transfer the mix to a blender, reserving some of the liquid and blend until smooth (you are looking for soup consistency, add remaining liquid if needed). Check the seasoning and pass through a fine sieve.

To Assemble

Preheat the oven to 180ºC (fan).

Place a large, non-stick frying pan onto a medium heat. Add the oil and place the seasoned fish, skin-side down, into the pan. Cook for 2-3 minutes, then transfer the pan to the oven for 6-10 minutes or until cooked through.

Cook the asparagus in boiling water for 1-2 minutes and wilt the greens in a little butter and salt. Remove from the pan and sit on kitchen paper to remove any excess liquid. Warm the courgette sauce, adding the mussels at the last minute to warm through. Place the wilted greens and asparagus onto the plate followed by the mussels. Sit the fish on top of the vegetables. Serve the courgette sauce in jugs and pour around the fish to serve.

Chef's Tip

This dish can be adapted to a great vegetarian offering. Exclude the fish and shellfish and try chargrilling the courgette before starting the sauce. Add some fresh peas to the asparagus and greens for a fresh, flavoursome soup.

MASCARPONE PANNA COTTA, BLACKBERRIES, OATS & CUCUMBER

SERVES 4

*Klein Constantia, Vin de Constance, Constantia
2006 (South Africa)*

Ingredients

Cucumber Sorbet (Serves 8)

150g caster sugar
150ml water
25g liquid glucose
¼ lemon (juice of)
1½ cucumbers

Mascarpone Panna Cotta

400g mascarpone cheese
400ml double cream
200ml semi-skimmed milk
115g caster sugar
4 leaves gelatine (soaked in cold water)

Oat Clusters

250g porridge oats
50g unsalted butter
1 tsp honey
salt (pinch of)

To Serve

24 blackberries
edible flowers

Method

For The Cucumber Sorbet (Prepare ahead)

Bring the sugar, water and glucose to the boil in a saucepan. Once boiling, add the lemon juice. Remove from the heat and leave to cool in the fridge. Juice the cucumbers in a juicer. Add the juice to the chilled sorbet base and churn in an ice cream machine until it reaches a sorbet consistency. Store in the freezer until needed (preferably do this the day before).

For The Mascarpone Panna Cotta

Warm the mascarpone, cream, milk and sugar in a pan over a low to medium heat until all combined. Take off the heat, add the soaked, squeezed out gelatine, mix well and pour into a container or mould. Chill and set in the fridge for at least 4 hours.

For The Oat Clusters

Gently heat the oats in a saucepan over a low-medium heat until very lightly toasted. Add the butter and honey and mix well. Continue to cook for a further 30-60 seconds. Remove from the heat and pour onto greaseproof paper, moving the mixture to form small clusters. Leave to cool.

To Assemble

Cut or spoon out pieces of the panna cotta and arrange onto the plate. Place on some of the oat clusters followed by the blackberries. Finally, *quenelle* the cucumber sorbet and place onto the dish. Use some of the oats as a bed to stop the sorbet moving about.

Chef's Tip

This dish can be adapted to any seasonal offerings. Keep the panna cotta and oat clusters as a base and alter the fruit and sorbet flavourings; chocolate and orange is a winner.

RESTAURANT 1861

Cross Ash, Abergavenny, NP7 8PB

0845 388 1861 or 01873 821 297
www.18-61.co.uk Twitter: @1861Restaurant

Simple, unfussy flavours are to the fore at Restaurant 1861, where chef-proprietor Simon King makes the most of seasonal ingredients.

The acclaimed chef's background as a chef under Michel Roux Senior at the 3 Michelin starred Waterside Inn, is evident in his elegantly presented food.

Simon has a magnificent larder on his doorstep and is able to make the best of seasonal produce from Monmouthshire, as well as the freshest ingredients from his own garden.

"We are fortunate to be located in an area of exceptional produce," says Simon, "we bring classic combinations to the table that showcase immaculate local ingredients."

Simon spent three years at the Waterside Inn before spending a further seven years at the 2 Michelin starred Restaurant Lettonie, with Martin Blunos.

He took a head chef's position at Llansantffraed Court Hotel before becoming chef-proprietor at 1861. His wife, Kate, dedicates herself to the front of house and an ever expanding wine list, while Simon is firmly in control of the kitchen.

Restaurant 1861 is a family business and Simon and Kate's two children live with them on the premises. Kate's father supplies most of the kitchen's fruit and vegetables.

Simon enjoys twice daily deliveries, with salads, herbs and vegetables stunningly fresh. His dishes change with the seasons and guests enjoy his flavoursome food in a light and spacious dining room. Simon's experience is reflected in every dish, with sophisticated combinations making the best of ingredients. He says: "We enjoy food that is elegant and reflects the flavours of Monmouthshire."

Restaurant 1861 offers a fabulous fine dining experience, well worth going the extra mile for!

Built
BY
James Williams
1861

COURGETTE FLOWERS STUFFED WITH GOAT'S CHEESE, BEETROOT COULIS

SERVES 4

 Château De Brau, Pure Viognier 2013 (France)
A light, fresh and fruity organic wine.

Ingredients

Beetroot Coulis

1 large onion (peeled, diced)
500g beetroot (peeled, diced)
caraway seeds (pinch of)
salt, pepper and sugar (to season)
500ml water

Batter

100g self-raising flour
salt (pinch of)
100ml cold water

Courgette Flowers

300g soft, creamy goat's cheese
8 courgette flowers (trimmed, stamens removed)
salt (to season)

Method

For The Beetroot Coulis

Place the diced onion in a heavy-based pan and sweat gently until translucent. Add the beetroot and caraway seeds, then season lightly with the salt, pepper and sugar. Add the water, bring to the boil and simmer gently until the beetroot is cooked through. Transfer to a liquidiser and blend to a smooth coulis. Strain through a fine sieve and adjust seasoning to taste. Reserve and keep warm.

For The Batter

Sieve the flour into a bowl with the salt. Pour in the water and whisk thoroughly to a smooth batter. Set aside for 10 minutes.

For The Courgette Flowers

Soften the goat's cheese at room temperature for 30 minutes before use. Place into a piping bag with a large nozzle. Open the courgette flowers and pipe the goat's cheese inside. Twist the flower closed to prevent the cheese from escaping. Repeat until all of your flowers are filled with the cheese. Coat the flowers in the batter and deep fry (180ºC) for 3-4 minutes until crisp and golden and the courgette is cooked through. Drain on a piece of kitchen towel and season with salt.

> **Chef's Tip**
>
> Blow into the courgette flowers to open them up gently to check for any insects!

To Serve

Spoon the beetroot coulis into the centre and carefully place the courgettes onto each plate.

FILLET OF HAKE, CHAMPAGNE & CHIVE CREAM

SERVES 4

Barone Pizzini Verdicchio, Classico Superiore, 2014 (Italy)
Organic and vegan, smooth, dry and fruity to combat the richness of the cream.

Ingredients

Champagne & Chive Cream

250ml Champagne
250ml fish stock
200g fish trimmings
1 lemon (rind of)
500ml double cream
salt and pepper (to season)
1 bunch chives

Chive Oil

1 bunch chives
100ml rapeseed oil
salt (pinch of)

Hake

500ml fish stock
4 x 150g hake fillets
salt (pinch of)
lemon juice (spritz of)

To Serve

selection of your favourite seasonal vegetables

Method

For The Champagne & Chive Cream

Pour the Champagne into a deep pan, bring to the boil and reduce by half. Add the fish stock and fish trimmings. Peel a couple of strips of rind from the lemon, add to the pan, bring back to the boil and reduce the liquid by half again. Add the cream, return to the boil and simmer gently for 10 minutes or until a light, creamy sauce consistency is achieved. Season to taste, strain into a clean pan and keep warm. Snip the chives into a separate bowl.

For The Chive Oil

Cut the chives into 2cm long pieces, then place into a liquidiser with the oil and salt. Process until smooth, strain through a sieve and reserve.

For The Hake

Bring the fish stock to the boil, then reduce the heat so that the stock is just bubbling lightly. Season the hake portions and place into the fish stock. Poach gently for 6-8 minutes or until cooked through. Remove from the stock, squeeze on a little lemon juice and keep warm.

> **Chef's Tip**
> Squeeze some lemon juice onto the fish when serving, it will really lift the flavour.

To Serve

Arrange the cooked vegetables on the plate. Heat the sauce and stir in the chives, then spoon neatly over and around the dish. Place a piece of fish onto each plate and finish with a drizzle of the chive oil.

ELDERFLOWER PANNA COTTA WITH POACHED GOOSEBERRIES

SERVES 6

🍷 *Paul Cluver, Riesling, Noble Late Harvest 2014
(South Africa)
Delicious and light, without the cloying of some
dessert wines.*

Ingredients

Poached Gooseberries

500g gooseberries
250g caster sugar
lemon juice (spritz of - optional)

Elderflower Panna Cotta

250ml double cream
250ml semi-skimmed milk
3 large elderflower heads
65g caster sugar
2 leaves bronze gelatine (soaked in cold water)

Elderflower Fritters

250ml cold water
225g plain flour
2 eggs
50ml white wine vinegar
salt (pinch of)
50g caster sugar
oil (to deep fry)
6 large elderflower heads
vanilla sugar (to sprinkle)

6 dariole moulds or ramekins

Method

For The Poached Gooseberries (Prepare ahead)

Toss the gooseberries in the sugar and place in the
fridge overnight.

Place the gooseberries in a pan with the sugary syrup and
heat until almost boiling. Add more sugar or a squeeze of lemon
juice to taste. Leave to cool.

For The Elderflower Panna Cotta

Place the cream, milk, elderflowers and sugar in a pan and heat
gently for 30 minutes to infuse the elderflowers. Remove from
the heat and leave to stand for a further 30 minutes, thus
ensuring maximum flavour.

Place the pan over a low heat, add the gelatine and stir until
dissolved. Allow to cool slightly.

Strain the mixture through a fine sieve and pour into moulds or
ramekins. Refrigerate for 4 hours to set.

Chef's Tip

You can adapt the flavour of the panna cotta by simply using
a different flavour infusion. Why not try cinnamon and serve
with warmed blackberries in the autumn?

For The Elderflower Fritters

Mix the water and flour together, add the eggs and mix until
you have a smooth batter, then add the vinegar, salt and sugar.

Heat the oil to 170°C. Check the elderflowers are free of wildlife
and are clean.

Coat each elderflower head in batter and fry in the hot oil
until crisp and golden. Drain from the oil, remove any excess
stalk and sprinkle with vanilla sugar.

To Serve

Dip each panna cotta, still in the mould, into warm water for a
few seconds to help it release. Turn out onto the centre of the
plate and arrange the poached gooseberries around. Place the
fritter alongside the panna cotta.

166
RESTAURANT JAMES SOMMERIN

The Esplanade, Penarth, CF64 3AU

02920 706 559
www.jamessommerinrestaurant.co.uk
Twitter: @RestaurantJS Facebook: Restaurant James Sommerin

Restaurant James Sommerin, located on the idyllic coastline of Penarth, is a fine dining restaurant with a relaxed ambience. Unfussy and unpretentious, it showcases the best of Welsh and British ingredients.

Food and great wine is at the heart of the dining experience. Customers can enjoy Sommerin's bespoke seasonally based menu or, for the more adventurous palates, the restaurant also offers a six or nine course tasting menu, with the option of a surprise tasting menu created for each table.

Every diner has a view of the stunning Penarth Estuary - even the chefs, who are able to enjoy the best of Mother Nature by looking through the glass-walled kitchen. Since opening in 2014, the restaurant has evolved with new décor throughout and has the addition of nine immaculate bedrooms above. Diners can now enjoy their dining experience without having to worry about getting home.

"Food is a family thing and the restaurant is for people of all ages; from children to grandparents," says James.

"I have always loved the idea that people come to sit down at a table and talk. It's for people of all ages and from all walks of life."

Keeping that 'family thing' in mind, you will find James' eldest daughter Georgia, in the kitchen alongside her dad, training to be a chef. "I wish I had as much talent and passion at 17 years of age as she does. My grandmother Eleanor inspired me and I like to think I have had a little of that inspiration with Georgia. I'm very proud!"

"Since opening in 2014, the restaurant has gone from strength to strength; 3 AA Rosettes, Restaurant of the Year for Wales at The Food Awards Wales and number 30 in the Good Food Guide. I am very proud of my team and my family. Without them my dream wouldn't be a reality." - James Sommerin.

PIGEON WITH BLACK PUDDING PUREE, BEETROOT & RASPBERRY DRESSING

SERVES 4

🍷 *Les Jardins, Pinot Noir, Domaine Léon Boesch, Alsace, 2014 (France)*

Ingredients

Black Pudding Purée

250g black pudding
30ml port
50ml chicken stock
30ml red wine vinegar

Raspberry Dressing

2 shallots (finely chopped)
1 clove garlic (finely chopped)
150ml rapeseed oil
1 bunch tarragon (finely chopped)
50ml sherry vinegar
1 punnet raspberries

Beetroot

1 large red beetroot
1 large golden beetroot
salt

Pigeon

2 pigeon breasts
1 tbsp rapeseed oil

Garnish

seasonal green leaves

Method

For The Black Pudding Purée

Place the black pudding, port and chicken stock in a pan and bring to the boil. Add the red wine vinegar and blend together. Pass through a fine sieve and set to one side.

For The Raspberry Dressing

Gently *sauté* the shallots and garlic in 50ml of the oil, then add the tarragon. Add the sherry vinegar and reduce by half. Remove from the heat and allow to cool slightly. Add the raspberries and remaining oil.

For The Beetroot

Preheat the oven to 200°C (fan).

Place the beetroot on a bed of salt in an ovenproof tray and cover with foil. Bake for 2 hours. Once cooked, peel, skin and dice.

To Finish & Assemble The Dish

Pan fry the pigeon breasts in oil for 1 minute on each side. Remove from the pan and allow to rest.

Using the same pan the pigeon was cooked in, add the beetroot with 1 tablespoon of raspberry dressing and gently warm. Add the rested pigeon breast and coat with the dressing. Remove from the heat and cut the pigeon breasts in half.

Swipe a spoonful of black pudding purée onto the plate and place the pigeon cut-side up.

Dress with the beetroot and raspberry dressing and garnish with seasonal green leaves of choice.

Chef's Tip

Don't overcook the pigeon. It is best served pink as it keeps the meat lovely and tender. Overcook and there is the risk of it being tough and it loses its lovely pink colour.

LAMB WITH BROAD BEANS, ASPARAGUS & TARRAGON

SERVES 4

 Domaine de Ferrand, Côtes du Rhône, 2011 (France)

Ingredients

500g lamb loin (skinned, fat removed)

Jus

2 shallots (thinly sliced)
oil (drizzle of)
1 tsp cumin seeds
100ml Madeira
500ml lamb stock
20g butter

Tarragon Crème Fraîche

1 bunch tarragon (finely chopped)
250g crème fraîche
1 lemon (juice of)

Turnip Purée & Slices

4 turnips (preferably pink, peeled)
whole milk (to cover)
50g butter
salt (to sprinkle)

Asparagus

100g butter
50ml water
1 bunch asparagus

To Serve

½kg broad beans
1 punnet nasturtium leaves

Method

To Cook The Lamb

Seal the loin of lamb for 3 minutes on each side and allow to rest.

> **Chef's Tip**
>
> For added flavour, marinate the lamb loin in olive oil and rosemary for 1 hour before cooking.

For The Jus

Lightly sauté the shallots in a little oil in a pan. Add the cumin seeds and *deglaze* the pan with Madeira. Pour in the lamb stock and reduce by half, then blend in the butter.

For The Tarragon Crème Fraîche

Mix the finely chopped tarragon with the crème fraîche and lemon juice.

For The Turnip Purée & Slices

Chop 3 of the turnips and place them in a pan. Cover with milk, add the butter and bring to the boil. Cook until soft.

Once cooked, drain and keep the liquid to one side. Place the turnips into a blender and gradually add the liquid to form a purée.

Thinly slice the remaining uncooked turnip and sprinkle with salt.

For The Asparagus

Place the butter and water in a pan and bring to the boil to melt and *emulsify* the butter. Trim the bottom of the asparagus, place into the pan and cook until the asparagus is just cooked.

For The Broad Beans

Pod the broad beans and *blanch* in boiling water for 2 minutes. Remove and cool in ice water. Pod again to remove the grey skin.

To Assemble The Dish

Preheat the oven to 180°C (fan).

Warm the loin in the oven for approximately 4 minutes – personal preference to length of cooking time required.

Warm the broad beans and asparagus through the *emulsion*. Place a swirl of tarragon crème fraîche onto the plate followed by a spoonful of turnip purée. Cut the loin, serving 2 pieces per person, and place on the plate. Arrange the broad beans and asparagus, followed by sliced turnip on top and nasturtium leaves to make the dish look pretty. Finish with the jus.

PEACH MELBA

SERVES 4

🍷 *'Mrs Wigley', Moscato, Wirra Wirra, McLaren Vale, 2014 (Australia)*

Ingredients

Peach Domes
200ml peach purée
2g agar agar

Frozen Raspberries
1 punnet raspberries

Vanilla Custard
5 egg yolks
100g caster sugar
200ml whole milk
200ml whipping cream
2 vanilla pods (split, scraped)

Honeycomb
200g caster sugar
90g golden syrup
15g bicarbonate of soda

Italian Meringue
100g caster sugar
40ml water
100ml liquid glucose
80g egg white

Raspberry Purée
2 punnets raspberries
50g caster sugar
20ml apple juice

Roasted Peaches
2 peaches
caster sugar (generous sprinkle of)

To Serve
1 punnet red vein sorrel

Chef's Tip
You need to work fast, handling the frozen domes needs to be kept to a minimum as they will melt very quickly. It can only be assembled when ready to serve. You really need an espuma can otherwise the custard is too heavy for the peach dome, causing it to fall apart.

Method

For The Peach Domes (Prepare ahead)
Bring the peach purée and agar agar to the boil, then remove from the heat.
Using the back of an oiled ladle, dip into the peach purée and freeze (this is a hard and time consuming process). Once frozen, remove from the ladle and gently place back in the freezer.
You will need 2 of these per person and they can be prepared up to 24 hours in advance.

For The Frozen Raspberries (Prepare ahead)
Freeze the raspberries, then break into pieces. Store in the freezer.

For The Vanilla Custard
Whisk the egg yolks and sugar together in a bowl.
Place the milk, cream and vanilla in a pan and bring to the boil. Pour into the egg mixture, whisking constantly. Return to the heat and thicken slightly. Remove, pass through a fine sieve and allow to cool. Place into a cream whipping canister (espuma can), charge with one gas charge and refrigerate.

For The Honeycomb
Combine the sugar and syrup together in a pan and boil to 140°C.
Add the bicarbonate of soda and gently shake the pan (do not mix), this will rapidly increase in size. Pour into a lined, heatproof bowl and allow to cool (be careful with this process as it is molten sugar and exceptionally hot!).

For The Italian Meringue
Combine the sugar, water and glucose in a pan and boil to 121°C.
Whilst this is coming up to temperature, whisk the egg white to a stiff peak in a separate bowl.
Gradually pour the glucose mixture into the egg white and whisk until cool.
Preheat the oven to 90°C (fan).
Spread the mix onto greaseproof paper and bake for 2-3 hours. Once baked and cooled, break into shards.

For The Raspberry Purée
Bring the raspberries, sugar and apple juice to the boil, then blend and pass through a fine sieve.

For The Roasted Peaches
Preheat the oven to 180°C (fan).
Cut the peaches into 8, sprinkle generously with sugar and bake for 10 minutes. Leave to cool to room temperature.

To Assemble The Dish
Arrange the purée and roast peaches on a plate. Layer with frozen raspberry pieces, meringue and sorrel. Remove the domes from the freezer and fill half with the aerated vanilla custard and lay the other half of the dome on top. Place on top of the other elements on the plate and serve immediately.

176
SOSBAN & THE OLD BUTCHER'S RESTAURANT

1 High Street, Menai Bridge, Isle of Anglesey, LL59 5EE

01248 208 131
www.sosbanandtheoldbutchers.com Twitter: @The_oldbutchers

Young husband and wife team Stephen and Bethan Stevens ventured into the restaurant industry in 2012. Both gave up their employment and took a leap of faith - to produce excellent food using the best locally sourced ingredients. The goal was to create a relaxed dining environment for local customers to enjoy creative, innovative dishes, with flavour being paramount.

Four years later, Sosban and The Old Butcher's has a loyal, local customer base and its reputation is now nationwide. They have created what is considered a 'destination restaurant' located in the heart of Menai Bridge, on the Isle of Anglesey, within a historical butcher's shop.

The restaurant itself is modestly furnished having sourced the majority of the woodwork from a local carpenter, Tom Vousden. Tableware includes pieces from the nearby slate mine, Penrhyn, Bethesda.

The original slate wall transports you to the days of the old butcher's shop. Artwork is created by the well-known Welsh artist, Mary Lloyd Jones. "There is a true sense of place here, unlike no other, historically rooted within our vibrant town, which is fast becoming the 'foodie' town of North Wales," states Bethan.

Sosban holds 3 AA Rosettes and provides a unique dining experience. Chef Stephen creates a series of dishes using the best, locally sourced produce available each day, offering customers a culinary journey not to be found anywhere else.

As well as holding 3 AA Rosettes, Sosban and The Old Butcher's was awarded 'Best Restaurant North Wales' in the Welsh Food Awards 2016 and 'Best Local Restaurant' in the 2017 edition of The Waitrose Good Food Guide.

UMAMI LOG

SERVES 4

 Crianza Pinot Grigio
(Italy)

Ingredients

Kale & Dressing
8 whole kale leaves (washed, dried)
clarified butter (to brush)
1 clove garlic (finely grated)
1 tsp Dijon mustard
1 tsp Worcestershire sauce
2 tbsp lemon juice
ground black pepper (to season)
1 egg, 200ml olive oil
4 anchovy fillets (finely chopped)
Parmesan (to dust)

Brine
250g Maldon sea salt
100g Demerara sugar
1 tbsp whole black peppercorn
5 cloves
2 litres water

Chicken Wings
12 chicken wings
buttermilk (to cover)

Pasta Straws
200g 00 grade pasta flour
2 large free range eggs

Cheddar Paste
25g unsalted butter
25g plain flour
400ml whole milk
salt and white pepper
125g Cheddar cheese (grated)

Chicken Skin & Bacon
4 rashers smoked bacon
100g chicken skin

Spice Mix
150g plain flour, 50g cornflour
1 tbsp chilli powder, 2 tsp garlic powder
1 tsp smoked paprika, 1 tsp sweet paprika
1 tsp dried oregano
1 tsp dried marjoram
1 tsp dried basil

Method

For The Kale & Dressing (Prepare ahead)
Brush the kale leaves with *clarified* butter and place in a dehydrator on high, or in a very low oven, for at least 8 hours.

Combine the garlic, mustard, Worcestershire sauce, lemon juice, pepper and egg in a bowl with a whisk. Gradually whisk in the oil until *emulsified*. Finally whisk in the chopped anchovies.

For The Brine & Chicken Wings (Prepare ahead)
Bring the brine ingredients to the boil until the salt and sugar are dissolved. Leave to cool.

Marinate the wings in the cold brine for 1 hour, then drain. Store in the fridge immersed in buttermilk until required.

For The Pasta Straws
Mix the flour and eggs to a crumb in a processor. Knead by hand for 10 minutes to a smooth dough. Cover with cling film and refrigerate for 30 minutes. Run through a pasta machine on the spaghetti setting.

For The Cheddar Paste
Melt the butter in a saucepan. Stir in the flour and cook out for 1-2 minutes. Off the heat, gradually stir in the milk to make a smooth sauce. Simmer gently for 8-10 minutes and season with salt and white pepper. Stir in the cheese until melted. Cool.

For The Chicken Skin & Bacon
Preheat the oven to 200°C (fan).

Place the chicken skin and bacon on a tray and roast for 10 minutes, or until crisp. Leave to cool, then chop to a fine crumb.

To Assemble The Dish
Remove the chicken wings from the buttermilk and coat in the spice mix. Deep fry (180°C) for 4 minutes, then drain on kitchen cloth.

Place the spaghetti straws in the fryer then carefully, with tweezers, remove and allow to cool.

Spread the cheddar paste along the pasta straws, then dip into the chicken and bacon crumb.

Dress the kale with the prepared dressing. Finish with grated Parmesan. Serve all 3 elements together as pictured.

> **Chef's Tip**
> Dot crème fraîche on the chicken wings to serve, this will provide a lovely contrast.

SAVOURY ETON MESS

SERVES 4

🍷 Domaine du Poujol Rosé, IGP de l'Hérault, 2014 (France)

Ingredients

Beetroot Powder
300g beetroot (cooked)
100ml beetroot juice
2g xanthan gum
seasoning

Meringue
100ml beetroot juice
1g xanthan gum
1g Hy-foamer

Pistachios
4 tbsp pistachios
25g icing sugar
salt (pinch of)

Beetroot
6 fresh beetroot (cooked)
unsalted butter (knob of)
seasoning

Garnish
20 fresh raspberries
100g live yoghurt

Method

For The Beetroot Powder (Prepare ahead)

Blend the cooked beetroot with the beetroot juice and whilst whizzing, add the xanthan gum to thicken. Season to taste. Pour onto a non-stick mat. Place in a dehydrator overnight. Once set to a crisp, grind in a spice grinder to a fine powder. Set aside in an airtight container until required.

For The Meringue (Prepare ahead)

Whisk the beetroot juice, xanthan gum and Hy-foamer in a stand mixer until the meringue ribbons up the whisk. Spread out evenly onto a non-stick mat and dehydrate for 6 hours.

For The Pistachios

Place the pistachios in a pan over a medium heat. Add the sugar and salt and keep stirring until the nuts are coated in sugar and roasted. Set aside to cool.

To Assemble The Dish

Ball the beetroot using a melon scoop. Warm in a pan with butter and season. Place in the centre of the plate. Scatter the raspberries and pistachios. Dot the yoghurt on the raspberries and beetroot, sieve over some of the beetroot powder and carefully finish with the shattered meringue.

Chef's Tip

Cook beetroot as you would potatoes; try to select similar sized beets. They are ready when the beetroot falls off the skewer when tested. We used white beets in this recipe.

RHUBARB & CUSTARD

SERVES 8

 Riesling Dessert Wine (New Zealand)

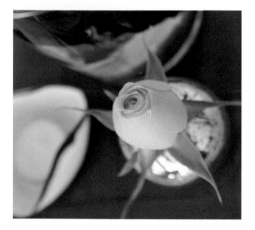

Ingredients

Custard

1 vanilla pod (scraped)
250ml whole milk
3 egg yolks
62g caster sugar
80g plain flour
200ml whipping cream (optional)

Almonds

125g flaked almonds
75g unsalted butter
6 tbsp tapioca maltodextrin
salt

Rhubarb Purée & Batons

300g rhubarb (washed, cut into batons)
150g caster sugar

Puffed Rice

small pan of veg oil
wild rice (handful of)

To Serve

1 sprig lemon thyme (picked)

Method

To Make The Custard

Place the vanilla pod and seeds in a heavy-based saucepan with the milk and bring to the boil.

Mix the yolks and sugar in a bowl for a few seconds, sift in the flour and mix again.

Pour the just-boiling milk over the yolk mixture, whisking constantly to prevent curdling, then return the mixture to the saucepan. Cook over a medium heat, whisking constantly for about 5 minutes, until very thick.

Pass through a fine sieve, discarding the vanilla, and place a sheet of cling film on the surface of the custard to prevent a skin forming. Leave to cool, then refrigerate. Place in an espuma gun and charge twice. Alternatively, whip the whipping cream and mix into the custard with an electric whisk. This will lighten it and provide an aerated effect.

For The Almonds

Preheat the oven to 180°C (fan).

Heat the almonds and butter over a medium heat, then place in the oven to roast for 3-4 minutes. Stir occasionally to ensure an even roast on the almonds. Allow to cool.

Once cooled, gradually add the tapioca and, using a whisk, combine into the almonds; the tapioca will absorb the butter, creating a soil effect. Season with salt to taste.

For The Rhubarb Purée & Batons

Divide the rhubarb and sugar evenly between 2 vac pack bags. Vac pack down and cook in a water bath at 65°C for 15 minutes. Quickly place in ice water to retain freshness. Purée half of the rhubarb in a food processor. Alternatively, poach the rhubarb until tender with a *cartouche* over it to lock in the flavour.

For The Puffed Rice

Heat the oil in a pan to 240°C. Drop the rice in and strain through a sieve. Set aside until needed.

To Assemble The Dish

Place the almonds in the base of the bowl. Scatter the puffed rice over. Sprinkle with a few lemon thyme leaves. Dot the rhubarb purée over and place the rhubarb batons evenly. Carefully, spoon the whipped custard onto the plate or fill a sphere using the espuma gun with the custard mix. Place down on the dish and serve immediately.

> **Chef's Tip**
> We serve aerated custard in spheres made from Isomalt, as pictured (see how to make them on page 226). The dish also works well with custard with added whipped cream.

186
STEAK ON SIX

Celtic Manor Resort, Coldra Woods, Newport, NP18 1HQ

01633 410 262
www.celtic-manor.com/steak-on-six Twitter: @TheCelticManor

An exciting dining destination for those seeking exquisite food in equally luxurious surroundings, few places are likely to create more of a lasting impression than Steak on Six.

Specialising in succulent steaks, the restaurant prides itself on showcasing the very best produce from around the British Isles and beyond, offering a creative culinary concept with a relaxed flavour. Alongside the finest speciality steaks, diners can also take their pick from an array of other fine meats and fresh fish, all grilled to perfection.

Steak on Six opened at the end of 2015 at Celtic Manor to complement the new Signature Collection of refurbished bedrooms and suites at the renowned 5 star resort. Diners can enjoy pre-dinner drinks including some specially-created cocktails in the exclusive Signature Lounge. The restaurant name points to its unique location and the spectacular elevated setting on the sixth floor of the Resort Hotel, meaning the dining room is flooded with light from a glass-walled terrace with beautiful views over the Coldra Woods during daylight. The setting also provides an intimate and enchanting dining experience into the evening hours.

Similar care and attention has been paid to the interior look with cow hide to be found on the chairs, bar and doors, reflecting the menu's focus on steak.

The restaurant takes its steak knives seriously with diners getting the chance to hand pick their 'weapon' from a varied collection offered for their perusal at the table.

The service team for this new restaurant has also been hand-picked from the resort's other seven restaurants and the kitchen output has been led by Celtic Manor's executive chef Michael Bates and resort head chef Simon Crockford. The standard of cooking and service therefore carries the highest expectations and the results have not disappointed with Steak on Six winning 2 AA Rosettes within six months of opening.

Specialising in succulent steaks, the restaurant prides itself on showcasing the very best produce from around the British Isles and beyond, offering a creative culinary concept with a relaxed flavour.

TEXTURES OF CAULIFLOWER WITH BUTTER POACHED LANGOUSTINE & CURED SCALLOP

SERVES 4

🍷 *Churton Sauvignon Blanc, Marlborough, 2012 (New Zealand)*

Ingredients

Cured Scallops
2 large hand-dived scallops
1 lime (zest of), 1 lemon (zest of)
50g sugar, 50g Maldon sea salt
3g coriander seeds, 3g fennel seeds

Langoustines
250g butter
4 large fresh langoustines (peeled, vein removed, reserve shells)
3 sprigs thyme, 2 cloves garlic
salt and freshly ground black pepper

Cauliflower Mousse
200g cauliflower (thinly sliced)
50g unsalted butter, 100ml whole milk
100ml water, 250ml double cream
2½ leaves gelatine (soaked in cold water)

Granola
25g pumpkin seeds, 30g almonds
10g sunflower seeds, 75g oats
25g butter, 5ml maple syrup, 2g thyme

Pickled Cauliflower
50ml water, 50ml white wine vinegar
50g sugar, 2g mustard powder
2g turmeric, 2 cloves, 2 star anise, 1 bay leaf
16 small cauliflower florets

Shellfish Bisque
langoustine shells and heads
20ml sunflower oil, 50g shallots
1 clove garlic, 30g celery, ½ bulb fennel
2g fennel seeds, 2g coriander seeds, 50g tomatoes
20g tomato purée, 80ml white wine, 15ml brandy
120ml fish stock, 50ml double cream
salt and pepper

To Finish & Serve
4 large cauliflower florets
4 cauliflower leaves, oil (to deep fry)
40g capers (deep fried), edible flowers

Method

For The Cured Scallops
Clean, trim and cut the scallops in half, then lay flat on a tray. Blitz the remaining ingredients together in a blender to make a cure. Allow the scallops to cure for a minimum of 3 hours in the fridge. Wash the cure off and keep in the fridge until ready to serve.

For The Langoustines
Clarify the butter to separate the milk solids. Remove the clear butter and keep at 55ºC. Add the thyme and garlic. Very gently cook the langoustines for 14 minutes. Remove from the butter and season with salt and pepper.

For The Cauliflower Mousse (Prepare up to 24 hours ahead)
Cook the cauliflower in the butter, then add the milk and water. Simmer until soft, then purée and strain through a fine sieve. Season to taste and allow to cool. Weigh out 300g.

Heat 50ml of cream and dissolve the gelatine into it. Whip the rest of the cream to a very soft peak. Whisk the warm cream into the purée, then fold in the whipped cream. Set in the fridge.

For The Granola
Preheat the oven to 160ºC (fan).

Pulse the seeds and almonds in a blender. Combine with the oats on a baking tray and bake for 18 minutes, turning regularly. Once coloured, remove from the oven and cool slightly. Melt the butter, mix with maple syrup and add the thyme. Coat all the ingredients and leave to set in clusters.

For The Pickled Cauliflower (Prepare up to 24 hours ahead)
Bring the water, vinegar, sugar and spices to the boil. Remove from the heat and allow to cool slightly, strain, then add the florets. Store in the fridge.

For The Shellfish Bisque
Roast the shells and heads in a little oil in a large pot until darker in colour. Add the chopped shallots, garlic, celery, fennel bulb, fennel and coriander seeds and the tomatoes. Roast over a high heat for 5 minutes until the shallots start to colour. Stir in the tomato purée and cook for a few minutes. *Deglaze* the pan with the wine, add the brandy and cook for a few more minutes. Add the fish stock and bring to the boil. Strain the sauce into a smaller pot and reduce by half. Add the cream, bring to the boil, then reduce the heat. Check the seasoning.

To Finish & Serve
Slice 8 ½cm slices from the cauliflower florets and char in a hot, non-stick pan until caramelised. Deep fry the cauliflower leaves at 165ºC until crisp, then lay on kitchen towel. Serve as pictured, finishing with a drizzle of the shellfish bisque.

(see glossary)

RUMP STEAK, BEEF CHEEK CROQUETTE, PICKLED SHALLOTS, HERB BUTTER

SERVES 4

 Barolo, Serralunga d'Alba, Giovanni Rosso, Piedmont 2011 (Italy)

Ingredients

Beef Rump

2 x 550g Welsh rump steaks (diamond cut)
2 cloves garlic (minced), 2 sprigs thyme
30ml *clarified* butter or quality olive oil
salt and freshly ground black pepper

Braised Beef Cheek Croquettes

1 beef cheek, butter (knob of), 1 tbsp oil
1 bulb garlic (cut in half)
30g onions (chopped)
30g carrots (chopped), 50ml red wine
100ml top quality veal or beef stock
black pepper (to season)
50g shallots (chopped)
1 clove garlic (minced), 2 sprigs thyme
100g potatoes (peeled, quartered)
flour, egg, breadcrumbs (to *pane*)

Pickled Shallots

100ml white wine vinegar
100g sugar, 2 cloves, 1 star anise, 1 bay leaf
150g banana shallots (peeled, cut into ½cm thick rings)

Tomato Crisps

2 plum tomatoes
2 sprigs thyme, 1 sprig rosemary
2 cloves garlic, 10g fresh sage, 10g fresh parsley
25ml extra virgin olive oil
Maldon sea salt (pinch of)

Herb Butter

120g butter, 10g baby spinach, 10g parsley
10g watercress, 10g tarragon, 10g chives
1 garlic clove, 1 lemon (zest of)
salt and pepper (to taste)

To Serve

1 pack watercress (washed)

Method

For The Beef Rump (Prepare 24 hours ahead)
Place the beef rumps with the garlic, thyme and butter or oil into a vac pack bag and seal. Keep in the fridge overnight. Remove from the fridge at least 1 hour before cooking.
Preheat a water bath to 55°C and cook the rumps for 90 minutes. Remove from the water bath and bag, then cook in a large, flat, hot frying pan, sealing the outside. Allow to rest for 15 minutes. Alternatively, slow roast at 120°C (fan) for 40 minutes.

For The Braised Beef Cheek Croquettes
(Prepare up to 3 days ahead)
Preheat the oven to 110°C (fan).
Brown the cheek in a frying pan with the butter, oil and garlic bulb, then remove the cheek. Brown the onions and carrots, then *deglaze* with red wine and reduce. Place into a deep oven tray, cover with stock and braise for 12 hours.
Pick the cheeks out of the stock and pull while still warm. Season with pepper, pass the stock through a sieve and reserve. Sweat the shallots, garlic and thyme, add the potatoes and some of the stock. Simmer until the potatoes are cooked. Mash the potatoes and add to the picked cheeks. Reduce the rest of the stock to a glaze and add to the cheek mix. Mix together thoroughly.
Shape into 4 croquettes, 8cm x 3cm. Refrigerate until firm. *Pane* twice, then refrigerate until needed. Deep fry (170°C) for 4 minutes in sunflower or rapeseed oil until golden.

For The Pickled Shallots (Prepare ahead)
Boil the ingredients together, apart from the shallots, allow to cool, then pass through a sieve. Add the shallot rings and refrigerate for 24 hours. They will keep for up to 2 weeks.

For The Tomato Crisps (Prepare ahead)
Slice each tomato into 4 lengthways, discarding the ends. Blend the herbs and garlic with the olive oil until smooth. Brush on top of the tomato slices, sprinkle with salt and place in a dehydrator for 8 hours, or onto greaseproof paper on a tray in the oven at 75°C (fan) for a few hours. Keep checking and turning every hour.

For The Herb Butter (Prepare ahead)
Blend all the ingredients in a food processor. Roll to a sausage shape between 2 layers of cling film and refrigerate for a few hours. Cut into 2cm thick slices and remove the cling film just prior to serving.

To Assemble
Slice the rumps, season with sea salt and pepper and top with the herb butter. Mix the watercress with the pickled shallots using the liquid as a dressing. Plate as pictured.

CHOCOLATE, ORANGE & WHISKY WITH ORANGE SAUCE & WHITE CHOCOLATE SOIL

SERVES 4

 Port - Superior Ruby, LBV or Tawny, Pedro Ximenez, Tokaj, Willi Opitz Beerenauslese (Austria)

Ingredients

Whisky & Orange Sphere

100ml whisky (Penderyn)
150ml orange juice
18g Ultratex or 4g agar agar

Chocolate Cube

200g 70% dark chocolate
2 egg yolks
40g caster sugar
200ml double cream (whipped to soft peaks)
100ml orange chocolate spray

White Chocolate Soil

100g white chocolate
30g maltodextrin

Orange Sauce

200ml orange juice
3 star anise
½ vanilla pod (seeds of)
50g caster sugar
10g Ultratex or 2g agar agar

8 hemisphere moulds
4 x 5cm cube moulds

Chef's Tip

This recipe can be adapted if you do not like whisky; use either Malibu, pineapple juice or just orange juice. The chocolate can be set into different shape moulds and can be made ahead and frozen if required.

Method

For The Whisky & Orange Sphere (Prepare ahead)

Bring the whisky to the boil and cook for 3 minutes. Add the orange juice and allow to cool slightly.

Whisk in the Ultratex to form a gel. Pipe into the moulds and set in the freezer. Once set, put the 2 halves together by heating one side and pressing together. Keep in the freezer.

If using agar agar: soak in some water and leave to stand for 10 minutes, then add to a little of the boiled, but slightly cooled whisky mixture and stir. Add the rest of the agar agar and bring back to the boil stirring constantly. Remove from the heat and fill the moulds.

For The Chocolate Cube (Prepare ahead)

Melt the chocolate in a *bain-marie* and leave to cool.

Place the egg yolks and sugar in a bowl over gently boiling water. Make a *sabayon* by whisking constantly, until it has increased in volume and forms peaks on the whisk.

Fold the egg mix into the chocolate with a wooden spoon, then fold in the whipped cream. Pipe the mix halfway into 5cm cube moulds. Place an orange and whisky sphere in the centre of each mould and fill to the top, ensuring the sphere is not protruding and the chocolate mixture is level with the moulds. Freeze. Remove from the freezer 12 hours before serving. Spray with orange chocolate spray when still frozen, then set on greaseproof paper and keep in the fridge.

For The White Chocolate Soil

Melt the white chocolate over a *bain-marie*. Allow to cool slightly. Add the maltodextrin to make the clusters, cool. Store in a sealed container in a cool place until ready to serve.

For The Orange Sauce

Bring the orange juice, star anise, vanilla seeds and sugar to the boil. Allow to cool, then add the Ultratex to make a gel. Refrigerate until ready to serve.

If using agar agar: soak in some water and leave to stand for 10 minutes. Add a little of the boiled, but slightly cooled mixture, stir, then add the rest. Bring back to the boil stirring constantly. Transfer to a container and cool. Once fully cooled it will set slightly, then use a hand blender to purée.

To Assemble

Put a spoonful of the orange sauce in the middle of the plate and spread it to make a circle. Cut a corner off the cube so it is flat, then place the cube onto the sauce. Sprinkle the soil on one side of the plate.

196
THE WALNUT TREE

Llanddewi Skirrid, Abergavenny, NP7 8AW

01873 852 797
www.thewalnuttreeinn.com Twitter: @lovewalnuttree

H e's one of Britain's greatest chefs. And though the classically-educated Shaun Hill could long since have retired, he still rattles the pans at the much-loved Walnut Tree, at Llanddewi Skirrid, near Abergavenny.

Hill is a masterful chef, a man whose intuitive understanding of great produce, balance and seasoning sets him apart from his contemporaries. He was described by Times critic Jonathan Meades as 'a truly great chef' - and few would disagree.

He began his career in 1966, working for Robert Carrier in his Islington restaurant, then moved to some of London's most prestigious addresses, including The Capital Hotel in Knightsbridge with Brian Turner and Blakes in South Kensington.

He won a Michelin star for Gidleigh Park in Devon where he was a key player in the Modern British food movement of the late 80s that fused local, seasonal produce with global influences.

His star rose further still when he moved to the pretty market town of Ludlow, in Shropshire. Hill was at the vanguard of another culinary boom; when Ludlow earned the nickname Gourmetville and had three Michelin starred restaurants in a town of just 10,000 people. It was here that his much missed 24-seat Michelin starred restaurant, The Merchant House, was hailed as the 14th best in the world, turning the Shropshire market town into a gastronomic destination.

Hill has taken a number of subsequent detours and now cooks at The Walnut Tree, where he was a regular customer when it was run by Franco Taruschio. He has enhanced its reputation since taking the reins in 2008.

Michelin starred Shaun Hill is an exceptional cook, ably supported by an impressive team. A visit to The Walnut Tree is essential for any serious fan of good food.

PEA SOUP WITH PORK PIE & PEAR CHUTNEY

SERVES 10

 Nuits–Saint-Georges (France)
or any good Pinot Noir

Ingredients

Pea Soup

6 shallots (peeled, chopped)
3 cloves garlic (crushed)
500g frozen peas
2 litres chicken stock
10 leaves fresh mint
50ml olive oil
250ml crème fraîche
salt and pepper

Pork Pie Pastry

100g lard, 100g butter
200ml hot water, 550g plain flour
2 medium eggs (plus extra for glazing)

Pork Pie Filling

1kg pork shoulder (cut into small cubes)
250g unsmoked streaky bacon (chopped small)
200ml hot water
250g fatty belly pork (minced)
12 sprigs sage (chopped)
1 tsp salt, 1 tsp mace
1 tsp ground black pepper
1 tsp ground white pepper
1 medium egg (beaten), 250ml meat stock
10 leaves gelatine (soaked in cold water)

Pear Chutney

125g tomatoes (chopped)
60g onion (peeled, chopped)
60g sultanas, 1 orange (juice of)
1 tbsp orange zest (coarsely chopped)
150g caster sugar
¼ tsp ground cinnamon
¼ tsp nutmeg
¼ tsp cayenne pepper
15g fresh ginger (chopped)
150ml white wine vinegar
saffron (pinch of), ½ tsp salt
375g pears (peeled, cored, cut into large dice)
60g cooking apple

loaf tin (or cake tin)

Method

For The Pea Soup

Heat the shallots, garlic and peas in the stock. Bring to the boil, then add the mint, olive oil and crème fraîche. Liquidise in a blender and season with salt and pepper.

For The Pork Pie Pastry (Prepare ahead)

Melt the lard and butter together in a pan with the water.

Mix the flour and eggs together in a separate bowl, then slowly incorporate the melted fat and water mix to form a dough. If the dough is a bit sticky then add a touch more flour.

Knead the dough a few times then wrap in cling film and rest in the fridge for 1 hour.

For The Pork Pie (Prepare ahead)

Preheat the oven to 180°C.

Combine all the filling ingredients, except the stock and gelatine, to form a stuffing.

Roll out two thirds of the pastry and line the loaf tin.

Fill this with the meat, then roll out the remaining pastry to make a lid and cover the meat. Make a small circular hole in the centre - best kept open during cooking with a little kitchen foil.

Brush with beaten egg and bake for 30 minutes, then lower the heat to 160°C and bake for a further 1¼ hours. Take out of the tin, brush with egg, then return to the oven for 10 minutes to brown.

Leave to cool and set for 1 hour. Make a jelly by warming the stock, then stirring in the gelatine.

When the pie is completely cold, pour in the cool, but not yet set, jelly and refrigerate overnight. This will bind the pastry to the filling so that the pie can be safely cut into wedges.

For The Pear Chutney

Mix all the ingredients, except the fruit, and bring to the boil. Simmer for 1 hour, stirring occasionally.

Add the pears and apple, then continue to cook for another 40 minutes. Store in Kilner jars.

To Serve

Serve as pictured.

Chef's Tip

This dish looks very simple but if you are planning to make all 3 components yourself, then it involves a bit of work - not worth embarking on for less than 10 portions.

STEAMED JOHN DORY WITH ORIENTAL SPICES

SERVES 4

Gewürztraminer
(Alsace, France)

Ingredients

John Dory

8 x 100g John Dory fillets
salt (pinch of)
Chinese five-spice (pinch of)
light sesame oil (to brush)
4 spring onions (cut into strips lengthways)

Dashi Broth

600ml dashi
1 thumb ginger (peeled, finely chopped)
1 tbsp coriander leaves
1 tbsp parsley leaves
2 spring onions (chopped)

To Finish

Japanese soy sauce (few drops of)

Method

For The John Dory

Skin the fish, then season with very little salt and a pinch of five-spice. Brush with sesame oil, then lay the spring onions on top and steam until done. This will take a few minutes, depending on the thickness of the fillets.

For The Dashi Broth

Warm the dashi with the ginger. Add the herbs and spring onions.

To Assemble The Dish

Carefully place the fish in bowls, then ladle the dashi broth on top. Finish with a dash of soy sauce.

Chef's Tip

I wouldn't suggest you make your own dashi with dried bonito tuna flakes and seaweed - you can buy the stock as a powder in oriental stores. Make the stock up as directed, then warm through with fresh herbs, coriander and parsley and spring onions to give a fresh taste. Add a few drops of Japanese soy sauce at the end to finish the broth.

STRAWBERRY TART

SERVES 4

🍷 *A light sweet wine, Austrian or German Trockenbeerenauslese, rather than deeply sweet Sauternes or Muscat.*

Ingredients

Sweet Pastry

250g plain flour
50g caster sugar
150g unsalted butter
1 medium egg

Pastry Cream

4 egg yolks
75g caster sugar
25g cornflour
300ml whole milk
2 vanilla pods (split)
30g unsalted butter
35ml double cream

Strawberry Ice Cream

250g strawberries (fully ripe)
50g caster sugar
125ml whipping cream

To Serve

16 ripe strawberries (hulled)
strawberry coulis

4 individual tart cases

Method

For The Sweet Pastry

Sieve the flour and sugar together. Rub in the butter and egg until it forms the texture of fine breadcrumbs. Squeeze together to form a ball of dough, then wrap in cling film and refrigerate for 1 hour. Roll out to 3cm thickness, then line 4 tart cases. Leave these in the freezer until needed.

Preheat the oven to 180°C.

Blind bake the pastry for 10 minutes. Crisp is the objective so cook until this happens if the pastry is still underdone. If the pastry starts to blister or rise during baking, then just pat it down with a clean cloth or kitchen paper.

For The Pastry Cream

Whisk the egg yolks, sugar and cornflour together. Bring the milk and vanilla pods to the boil, then whisk into the sugar, cornflour mix. Return this to the pan, add the butter and double cream and bring to the boil. Strain into a clean bowl and leave to cool.

For The Strawberry Ice Cream (Prepare ahead)

Hull the strawberries, then halve them. Process or blend with the sugar to make a purée. Separately whisk the cream into soft peaks, then fold in the fruit purée. Freeze. When the mix is half frozen, use a fork to mash together so that when it is completely set it will be an even consistency.

To Assemble The Dish

Spoon the pastry cream into the cooked tart cases. Slice the strawberries and lay on top.

Serve with a scoop of strawberry ice cream and any drops of strawberry juice or some strawberry coulis.

> **Chef's Tip**
>
> Strawberries are at their best in early summer. A drop of fraises des bois d'eau de vie in the pastry cream would be delicious but not completely necessary.

206
THE WHITEBROOK
RESTAURANT WITH ROOMS

Whitebrook, Near Monmouth, Monmouthshire, NP25 4TX

01600 860 254
www.thewhitebrook.co.uk Twitter: @TheWhitebrook @ChefChrisHarrod

The Whitebrook is a Michelin starred restaurant with eight rooms, set in the blissfully peaceful Wye Valley. In 2013 chef Chris Harrod followed his ultimate dream of owning his own restaurant with rooms and, within 11 months, The Whitebrook was awarded a Michelin star. It is also listed as one of the UK's Top 50 Restaurants in the 2017 edition of The Waitrose Good Food Guide.

Every dish served, from breakfast through to dinner, boasts locally sourced ingredients, many of which are foraged within a short distance from the restaurant. "It's all about putting the surrounding valley on the plate and we've really pushed that. In every dish, from the canapés to the petit fours and all the way through the meal, there's a connection to our surroundings and local ingredients," says Harrod.

Menus at The Whitebrook are bursting with exciting and unusual herbs garnered from the treasures of the surrounding forests and hedgerows, which elevates the dining experience to something very special indeed. Carefully selected wines are also recommended to complement each dish, championing local wines, independent growers, organic and biodynamic producers and lesser known grape varieties.

The Whitebrook delights all aspects of guests' senses, from the outstanding cuisine and visual appeal of the venue, to the pleasant and personal comfort of good service. The restaurant's natural stone and wood interiors provide a relaxed dining atmosphere and the simple but stylish furnished bedrooms are the epitome of a gastronomic rural retreat.

"I am always looking for vibrancy and freshness in the dishes we serve. I am so lucky to be surrounded by the best producers and that I am able to pick straight from my kitchen garden or forage the hedgerows just before service."
Chris Harrod.

WYE VALLEY ASPARAGUS, HOGWEED, MARITIME PINE, HEDGEROW PICKINGS, TINTERN MEAD

SERVES 4

 Shoreline, 2014, Lyme Bay, Axminster Devon (UK)

Ingredients

Pine Oil

20g flat-leaf parsley (washed, picked)
75g Maritime pine needles
75ml rapeseed oil

Asparagus

20 local asparagus spears (woody ends removed)
Maritime pine needles
100ml rapeseed oil
salt (pinch of)

Asparagus Purée

75g unsalted butter
250g asparagus (chopped)
4g salt

Hogweed

250g hogweed shoots
100g unsalted butter (diced)

Mead Sauce

125g mead (Parva Vineyard, Tintern)
7g honey
85g unsalted butter (diced)
salt (pinch of)
lemon juice (spritz of)
2g lecithin

Method

For The Pine Oil (Prepare ahead)

Cook the parsley for 6 minutes in boiling water, then strain and refresh in ice water. Squeeze dry. Place the pine needles, parsley and oil in a blender and blitz for 8 minutes. Strain into muslin cloth and hang above a bowl overnight.

For The Asparagus

Trim the asparagus to the same length and set aside. Reserve the trimmings for the purée.

For The Asparagus Purée

Melt the butter in a large saucepan. Add the asparagus, asparagus trimmings and season, cover and cook quickly until tender. Blend until smooth.

For The Hogweed

Pick the leaves and peel the shoots if stringy. *Blanch* the shoots for 2 minutes in boiling, salted water, then refresh in ice water. Fry the shoots and leaves in butter, adding more butter if they start to burn. The leaves will crisp as they caramelise. Season and strain on kitchen cloth.

For The Mead Sauce

Warm the mead, honey and butter, and whisk until *emulsified*. Add a little salt and lift with lemon juice. Add the lecithin and blitz until frothy.

To Serve

Preheat the oven to 180°C.

Place a bed of pine needles in a pan and lay the asparagus in a single layer on top. Coat with the rapeseed oil and season. Cover with foil and cook in the oven for 6 minutes until tender.

Warm the asparagus purée, stirring in a few drops of pine oil before placing it on the plate.

Place the asparagus and warmed hogweed shoots on the purée. Spoon the warm, frothed mead sauce over the asparagus. Sprinkle over the crisp hogweed leaves to finish.

Chef's Tip

Asparagus is around for a short time, from the end of April to the beginning of June. Take advantage and visit the nearest pick-your-own farms for the sweetest, freshest crop. At the restaurant we also forage pennywort and fiddle ferns to serve on the dish.

RYELAND LAMB, LOCAL GOAT'S CURD, HEIRLOOM COURGETTES, MALLOW, NASTURTIUM, BURNT ONION

SERVES 4

 Barbera d'Asti Superiore, 2012, Michele Chiarlo, Piemonte (Italy)

Ingredients

Lamb Shoulder

400g sea salt
8 cloves garlic
16 sprigs thyme
4 sprigs rosemary
4 bay leaves
8 black peppercorns
1 lamb shoulder (about 1.8kg)
30ml rapeseed oil
400ml water

Burnt Onion Powder

1 onion (peeled)

Mallow Purée

300g mallow leaves (chopped)
50ml water
2g salt

To Serve

12 heirloom courgettes (halved)
50ml extra virgin rapeseed oil
200g goat's curd
12 nasturtium leaves and flowers

Method

For The Lamb Shoulder (Prepare 2 days ahead)

Blitz the salt, garlic, herbs and spices to a powder. Place the lamb on a tray and rub with the salt mix. Wrap in cling film and refrigerate for 12 hours.

Preheat the oven to 150°C.

Wash the lamb thoroughly under cold running water and pat dry with a cloth.

Heat the rapeseed oil in a large roasting pan over a medium heat, add the lamb and colour for 7-10 minutes until golden. Take off the heat and remove any excess fat. Add the water, cover with foil and cook in the oven for 4½ hours, basting occasionally. Remove from the oven and allow to cool before removing the bones. For a neater presentation, wrap in cling film and press the shoulder between weighted trays in the fridge overnight. Cut into portions.

For The Burnt Onion Powder (Prepare 1 day ahead)

Separate the onion layers onto a tray and dry in a low oven (80°C) for 12 hours or overnight. Once dry, increase the temperature to 160°C and cook for 5-8 minutes until black. When cold, blitz to a fine powder.

For The Mallow Purée

Boil the mallow in unsalted water for 8 minutes. Drain, place in a blender with the water and blitz until smooth. Season.

To Serve

Place the lamb, fat-side down, in a pan and cook over a medium heat until golden and crispy. Fry the courgette halves, flesh-side down, until golden and just cooked. Season. Place the lamb and courgettes on an absorbent cloth.

Place 4 dots of goat's curd on each plate and sieve over the burnt onion powder. Top with the lamb and courgettes. Add 3 spoonfuls of mallow purée and scatter over the nasturtiums.

> **Chef's Tip**
>
> Instead of mallow you could substitute 300g spinach with 50g nasturtium leaves. Any cut of lamb could be used for the dish, for example grilled lamb cutlets. At the restaurant we also serve roasted lamb loin and crispy breast with the dish.

VIOLET PARFAIT, BLUEBERRIES, ROSE, LEMON THYME

SERVES 8

 Moscato d'Asti 'Palás', 2015, Michele Chiarlo, Piemonte (Italy)

Ingredients

Violet Parfait

100g caster sugar
30ml water
110g egg yolks
20ml whole milk
4½g gelatine leaf (soaked in cold water)
220ml whipping cream
6g violet essence
0.8g purple food colouring powder

Rose Jelly

100ml elderflower cordial
100ml water
4ml rose extract
5g gelatine leaf (soaked in cold water)

Blueberry Meringue

125g blueberry purée
12½g powdered egg white
2g citric acid
150g icing sugar
50g maltodextrin

Lemon Thyme Sorbet

250ml whole milk
250ml stock syrup
250ml lemon juice
10g lemon thyme

To Serve

200g blueberries
small lemon verbena leaves
viola flowers

8 individual parfait moulds

Method

For The Violet Parfait (Prepare ahead)

Combine the sugar and water in a pan and cook to 121°C.

Meanwhile in a mixer, whisk the egg yolks.

Heat the milk and dissolve in the gelatine.

When the syrup reaches 121°C, slowly pour onto the yolks whilst continuing to mix. Add the milk/gelatine and mix at high speed until cool.

Whip the cream to soft peaks.

Mix the violet essence and food colouring through the yolk mixture.

Add a third of the cream and mix well before carefully incorporating the rest of the cream.

Place into a piping bag. Pipe into the moulds and freeze until required.

For The Rose Jelly (Prepare ahead)

Heat the elderflower, water and rose extract in a pan, add the gelatine and dissolve. Pour into a shallow container and place in the fridge to set.

For The Blueberry Meringue (Prepare ahead)

Combine the purée, egg white and citric acid in a mixing bowl. Mix at high speed whilst slowly adding the sugar. Add the maltodextrin and leave to mix for 1 minute. Pipe onto a silicone sheet into mini tree branch shapes.

Dry in the oven at 65°C for 8 hours.

For The Lemon Thyme Sorbet (Prepare ahead)

Bring the milk, stock syrup and lemon juice to the boil, then remove from the heat. Add the lemon thyme and leave to infuse overnight. Strain and churn in an ice cream machine.

To Serve

Turn out the violet parfaits and place one on each plate. *Quenelle* the lemon thyme sorbet and sit it next to the parfait. Arrange the blueberries and pieces of rose jelly around. Carefully position the blueberry meringue branches before garnishing with small lemon verbena leaves and viola flowers.

> **Chef's Tip**
> Prepare all elements of this dish in advance.

216
WOLFSCASTLE
COUNTRY HOTEL

Wolfscastle, Near Haverfordwest, Pembrokeshire, SA62 5LZ

01437 741 225
www.wolfscastle.com Twitter: @staywolfscastle

Wolfscastle Country Hotel is situated in the village of Wolfscastle, only 10 minutes from the beautiful Pembrokeshire coastline, and has been synonymous with good food for decades.

In 2016, husband and wife team, Andrew and Mandy Stirling celebrated 40 years of ownership. Under their direction and hospitality, the hotel has developed into a haven of luxury and relaxation, with 2 AA Rosette cuisine.

"Passion for good food is something I grew up with," reminisces Andrew. "My parents owned the Hat and Feather in Knutsford, which in 1966 was voted one of the best 20 restaurants in Britain by the Good Food Guide."

This hunger for culinary excellence is highlighted by Wolfscastle's many accolades. As well as being awarded 2 AA Rosettes, it is a member of Welsh Rarebits - Hotels of Distinction, The Welsh Gold Collection of Hotels, Signpost – UK's Finest Hotels, Great Inns of Great Britain and has been awarded 4 star Country House Hotel status by Visit Wales & Historic Hotels of Britain.

The 'Allt-yr-Afon' Restaurant, along with the contemporary Brasserie, gives head chef Ian Wilson and his brigade of six plenty of scope to develop traditional as well as fine dining dishes. They have access to an abundance of fresh local produce in Pembrokeshire from both the land and sea, allowing them to create recipes that excite the palate.

"Ian has definitely raised our levels of culinary art to further heights. Being in his early thirties and having spent the last 17 years working in Switzerland, France and Britain, he has a wealth of knowledge and is an absolute joy to work with," says Andrew.

Wolfscastle Country Hotel is a haven of luxury, ideally located for exploring the beautiful Pembrokeshire coastline. Guests will enjoy a warm Welsh welcome and 2 AA Rosette cuisine in an ambience of perfect relaxation.

PENDERYN CURED SALMON

SERVES 10

 Grüner Veltliner 'Prager' Hinter Der Bury, 2014 (Austria)

Ingredients

Cured Salmon

1½-2kg side of salmon (pin boned)
200g sea salt flakes
200g Demerara sugar
75ml Penderyn whisky
1 blood orange (zest of)

Watercress Purée

300g watercress
200g spinach
1% xanthan gum

Garnish

1 blood orange (segments of)
2 tbsp dill (picked)
100ml crème fraîche

Method

For The Cured Salmon (Prepare ahead)

Clean the flesh of the fish with water and pat dry. Cut in half and place each half in a separate tray.

Mix all the other ingredients together in a bowl and divide the mix between the trays.

Turn the salmon twice a day so the cure is even. The tail piece can take as little as 2 days. The belly fillet may take up to 4 days.

Once cured, remove from the tray and gently wash under cold water. Pat dry then carefully rub a little oil onto the flesh. Portion as required. Use within 5 days or cling film and freeze.

Chef's Tip

Use grated beetroot to enhance the colour during the curing process.

For The Watercress Purée

Prepare a pan of slightly salted, boiling water and a pan of ice water.

Pick through the leaves before weighing to remove any large stalks or dirt.

Blanch the leaves for 40 seconds then submerge in the ice water. Scoop the leaves and some of the ice into a blender, weighing it as you do so.

Work out 1% of the total leaf and ice weight and weigh out the xanthan gum accordingly.

Blend the leaves and ice on high, occasionally opening the top to scrape the sides clean. Add the xanthan gum gradually with the blender on slow and stir and build the speed back up. After 1-2 minutes of blending, the purée can be passed through a fine sieve and used straight away.

To Assemble The Dish

Transfer the crème fraîche to a squeezy bottle. Arrange the elements as desired and garnish with blood orange segments and dill.

SALT MARSH LAMB & SCALLOPS

SERVES 4

*Côtes du Rhône 'In Fine' Vinsobres Domaine
Constant-Duquesnoy 2012, (France)*

Ingredients

Sea Beet Potato Cake

3 egg yolks
375g mashed potato (cold)
1 tbsp sea salt flakes
½ tbsp cracked black pepper
3 tbsp butter (soft)
110g sea beet or spinach (finely sliced)
4 egg whites

Lamb

1 salt marsh lamb shoulder (boned,
rolled, seasoned)
2 salt marsh lamb rumps (trimmed, seasoned)

Scallops

8 hand-dived scallops
salt and pepper

To Serve

1 pomegranate (seeds of)
1 radicchio lettuce (sliced)
4 spring onions (cut into 2cm lengths)
2 tbsp fresh mint (finely sliced)
200ml lamb or veal jus

20cm square baking tray (greased)

Method

For The Sea Beet Potato Cake

Preheat the oven to 175ºC (fan).

Mix the egg yolk and mashed potato to a smooth purée. Fold in the salt, pepper, butter and sea beet or spinach until well mixed.

Whip the egg whites to soft peaks. Stir in half the egg whites to the potato mix, then gently fold in the rest. Place in the prepared baking tray and bake for 25-30 minutes. Once cooled, cut into circles or squares as desired.

Chef's Tip

If unable to purchase sea beet, you can use spinach instead.

For The Lamb Shoulder (Prepare ahead)

Preheat the oven to 190ºC (fan).

Roast the seasoned lamb in a tray for 15 minutes until browned all over. Fill halfway up the side of the lamb with water.

Turn the oven down to 140ºC (fan).

Cover the lamb with tin foil and return to the oven for at least 4 hours or until soft like butter.

Once slightly cooled, remove the string and roll the lamb in heavy-duty cling film to form a cylinder. Cool in the fridge until needed.

For The Lamb Rump

Preheat the oven to 170ºC (fan).

Seal the rumps on all sides in a hot frying pan.

Place in the oven for 10-15 minutes, or until cooked as you like it. Rest in a warm place for 6 minutes.

For The Scallops

Prepare the scallops by removing any roe or skirt. Season lightly with salt and pepper.

Cook the scallops for 1 minute on each side in a hot frying pan. Put in a warm place to rest.

To Assemble The Dish

Preheat the oven to 175ºC (fan).

Place the cut potato cakes in the oven to warm through, about 10-15 minutes.

Slice the lamb shoulder into 3cm thick discs. Fry for 3 minutes on each side in a medium hot pan.

Place all the items on the plate as desired; a line of the items through the middle of the plate works nicely. Finish by pouring a little jus over the lamb and scallops.

CAFE GOURMANDE

SERVES 8

 Cava Albet i Noya, Reserva 21 Penedès, 2012 (Spain)

Ingredients

Chocolate Truffle Cake Sponge Base
50g egg yolks, 10g cocoa powder
50g butter (melted)
65g dark chocolate (melted)
75g egg whites, 100g caster sugar

Chocolate Mousse Filling
4 egg yolks, 50g caster sugar
230g dark chocolate (melted)
230g milk chocolate (melted)
568ml whipping cream (whipped to soft peaks)

Chocolate Mousse Topping
100g dark chocolate
50ml double cream, 25g butter

Orange Sorbet
275ml water, 175g caster sugar
6 oranges (juice of), 1 lemon (juice of)
50ml Grand Marnier

Fruit Jelly
1 sachet gelatine, 30ml warm water
450ml apple juice, 200g mixed berries

Sticky Date Tiramisu
130g mascarpone cheese
50ml Tia Maria, 25g caster sugar
1 vanilla pod (seeds of), 3 shots strong coffee
25ml Amaretto, 100ml butterscotch sauce
200g sticky toffee date pudding (cut into small squares)
250ml double cream (whipped)
cocoa powder (to dust), spun sugar (optional)

Fruit Tart
225g sweet pastry
500ml whole milk, 1 vanilla pod (split)
6 egg yolks, 120g caster sugar
50g plain flour, 2 tsp cornflour
berries (to decorate)

30cm x 21cm baking tin (greased)
8 shot glasses
8 x 4cm Kilner jars
8 x 4cm individual flan cases

Method

For The Chocolate Truffle Cake Sponge Base
Preheat the oven to 170°C (fan).
Whisk the egg yolks and cocoa powder together. Slowly pour in the butter while whisking, then add to the melted chocolate.
Make meringue with the egg whites and sugar, then fold into the chocolate mix. Spread onto the prepared baking tray and bake for about 8-10 minutes until firm to touch. Leave to cool.

For The Chocolate Mousse Filling
Whisk the eggs and sugar until doubled in size. Stir into the melted chocolates. Fold in the whipped cream, then spread on the sponge base.

For The Chocolate Mousse Topping
Gently melt all the ingredients together and pour on top of the mousse. Set in the fridge for 30 minutes. Portion when set.

For The Orange Sorbet (Prepare ahead)
Make a stock syrup with the sugar and water in a pan. Add the orange and lemon juice and Grand Marnier. Chill, then churn in an ice cream machine.

> **Chef's Tip**
> Adding a shot of Grand Marnier to the sorbet adds an extra twist to the flavour.

For The Fruit Jelly (Prepare ahead)
Melt the gelatine in the warm water. Stir in the apple juice, then pour into the shot glasses. Add the fruit and set for 3 hours in the fridge.

For The Sticky Date Tiramisu
Whisk the mascarpone cheese to soft peaks with half the Tia Maria, the sugar, vanilla seeds and 25ml of coffee.
To make the dipping liquid, combine the remaining coffee, Tia Maria and Amaretto.
Pour some butterscotch into the bottom of the Kilner jars. Soak the sticky toffee date pudding in the liquid and place in the bowl followed by the cream, repeat until full, about 2-3 layers. Dust with cocoa powder and adorn with spun sugar, if using.

For The Fruit Tart
Preheat the oven to 180°C (fan).
Line the flan cases with pastry and blind bake until golden, about 10-12 minutes. Leave to cool.
Bring the milk to the boil with the vanilla pod.
Whisk the yolks and sugar until pale. Add the flour and cornflour followed by the hot milk. Heat gently to a thick custard. Leave to cool. Add to the pastry base and chill. Decorate with the berries.

To Serve
Serve as pictured with an espresso, if desired.

HOW TO MAKE & BLOW SPHERES

Spheres (Makes 16, allow for breakages)

435g Isomalt refined sugar
35g water
gold metallic dusting powder (optional)

To Prepare The Isomalt (Prepare up to 2 days in advance, or on the day for a smoother sphere).

Heat the water in a medium saucepan over a medium heat. Carefully add in a little Isomalt, stirring occasionally with a spatula until it melts. Don't allow the Isomalt to touch the sides; keep the sides of the pan clean using a wet spatula.

Repeat, adding small amounts of Isomalt until all the Isomalt is melted.

Boil for at least 20 minutes until it reaches 165-171°C. Pour over a Silpat mat on a marble counter and leave to cool until the edges start to harden a little then, using protective gloves, fold the edges inwards. Repeat until all the Isomalt has been incorporated.

Knead the mixture by folding in half and letting it fall on itself. Repeat until the mix is cool enough to hold its shape, then start pulling and twisting it. Hold one end against the mat and pull the other end to stretch it, twist twice and fold it in half pressing the ends together. Repeat until you have a silky sheen, then pull twice without twisting. Cut with scissors into small, nugget-sized pieces. Store in a container with desiccant packets or over dry rice.

To Make & Blow The Spheres (Make on day of serving)

Warm the Isomalt pieces under a heat lamp. Knead and pull the Isomalt to even the temperature and create a smooth ball. It is very important to have the same temperature in all areas of the Isomalt to successfully blow a sphere.

With your index finger, push the Isomalt to create a hole making sure the thickness of the wall around the edges and bottom of the hole is the same.

Warm the edges of the hole over the flame of an alcohol burner and place it over the sugar blowing pump tube, ensuring it doesn't touch the bottom of the hole. You need an air pocket to be able to pump air.

Rhubarb & Custard, Sosban & The Old Butcher's Restaurant - **Page 184**

Holding the tube and Isomalt with one hand and holding the pump with the other, slowly start pumping air and rotating the Isomalt sphere to check that it is inflating evenly. Warmer areas will inflate more than colder areas.

To correct this, touch the warmer area with your hand to cool it down. Once the sphere has reached your desired size, cool it down using a fan or hair dryer on a cold setting.

To remove the sphere from the pump tube, warm up the Isomalt over the alcohol burner where it connects to the tube. Warm up the scissors and carefully cut the sphere from the tube. Place the sphere over a cloth or soft surface so it doesn't break when you cut it.

Clean the tube by warming it over the burner and pulling the remaining Isomalt out with scissors.

To cut a hole in the base of the sphere, warm up a small, round, metal cutter over the alcohol burner while you warm up the Isomalt sphere under the heat lamp or further away over the burner. Place the cutter on the counter facing upwards and carefully place the Isomalt sphere on top, with some slight pressure until you cut a hole. Brush the spheres with your choice of food colouring powder.

Store the spheres in a container with desiccant packets or over dry rice until serving time.

FISH

SWANSEA FISH LTD
Unit 5, Fisherman's Quay, Trawler Road, The Marina,
Swansea, SA1 1UN.
T: 01792 480 800
*Freshly caught fish direct to your dish. Supplied fresh
or frozen.*

WELSH SEAFOOD
The Docks, Milford Haven, Pembrokeshire, SA73 3AE.
T: 01646 692 331 www.welshseafoods.co.uk
*Suppliers of Welsh fish to local restaurants, building a
recognisable brand for fish caught in Welsh waters and
landed on Welsh shores.*

MERMAID SEAFOODS
Builder Street, Llandudno, Gwynedd LL30 1DR.
T:01492 878 014 E: enquiries@mermaidseafoods.co.uk
www.mermaidseafoods.co.uk
*One of the largest fish suppliers in Wales. For two
generations Mermaid Seafoods has been sourcing the best
fresh fish and seafood for North Wales restaurants, hotels
and private customers.*

MEAT

EYNON'S OF ST CLEARS LTD
Deganwy, Pentre Road, St Clears, Carmarthen, SA33 4LR.
T: 01994 230 226 www.cynons.co.uk
*Huw Eynon is one of the most skillful butchers in Wales
and his excellent shop and food hall should be a stop on
every foodie's itinerary on a visit to Carmarthenshire.*

HUNTSHAM COURT FARM
Huntsham Court, Ross-on-Wye, Herefordshire, HR9 6JN.
T: 01600 890 296 E: richard@huntsham.com
www.huntsham.com
*Richard Vaughan's farm produces some of the finest, rare
breed meats including pork, beef and lamb.*

T J ROBERTS & SON FAMILY BUTCHERS
Tryweryn House, 8 Station Road, Bala, Gwynedd, LL23 7NG.
T: 01678 520 471 www.welshqualitymeat.co.uk
*Excellent award-winning family butcher supplying local
Welsh black beef, pork and lamb.*

THE WELSH VENISON CENTRE
Bwlch, Brecon, Powys, LD3 7HQ.
T: 01874 730 929 www.beaconsfarmshop.co.uk
*Delicious free range venison and lamb situated in the heart
of the Brecon Beacons National Park. Family-run farm shop
since 1985.*

FINE FOOD & VEGETABLES

A DAVID & CO LTD
Hillside Farm, Sutton Wick, Bishop Sutton, Bristol, BS39 5XR.
T: 0330 333 4441 www.arthurdavid.co.uk
*A food service distribution company supplying the catering
industry for over 50 years.*

CASTELL HOWELL FOODS LTD
Cross Hands Food Park, Cross Hands, Llanelli,
Carmarthenshire, SA14 6S.
T: 01269 846 060 www.castellhowellfoods.co.uk
*Distributors of fine foods and local produce, working with
the best producers in Wales.*

JONES & DAVIES
Pontwelly, Llandysul, SA44 4AJ.
T: 01559 363 281 www.jonesanddavies.co.uk
Fresh produce specialists based in Llandysul, West Wales.

MEDWYNS OF ANGLESEY
Llanor, Old School Lane, Llanfair PG, Anglesey, LL61 5RZ.
T: 01248 714 851 www.medwynsofanglesey.co.uk
*Prize-winning vegetable seeds and plants. Medwyn
Williams MBE AHRHS FNVS - 11 times Gold medal winner
at the Chelsea Flower Show, Past Chairman of the Royal
Horticultural Society Fruit, Vegetable and Herb Committee
and President of the National Vegetable Society.*

RIVERSIDE MARKET GARDEN
Llantrithyd Road, Cowbridge, South Glamorgan CF71 7DP.
T: 07889 846 526 www.riversidemarketgarden.co.uk
*Suppliers of beautiful organic vegetables to Cardiff's
farmers' markets, restaurants, and local people (with a 'veg
box' scheme) for over three years.*

DAIRY

BIRCHGROVE EGGS
Trawscoed, Aberystwyth, Ceredigion, SY23 4AT.
T: 01974 261 286 www.birchgrove-eggs.co.uk
At Birchgrove they only have healthy and happy hens, with acres of land for them to roam and explore. They produce truly 'eggsellent' eggs so everyone's a winner! A family-run business supplying quality assured, Welsh free range eggs to a wide range of customers in Wales.

CALON WEN
Unit 8 West Wales Business Park, Redstone Road, Narberth, Pembrokeshire, SA67 7ES.
T: 01834 862 873 www.calonwen-cymru.com
The Welsh Organic Milk Co-op. An organic dairy co-operative of organic family farms, located all over Wales.

PERL LAS BLUE CHEESE
Caws Cenarth, Fferm Glyneithinog, Pontseli, Lancych, Carmarthenshire, SA37 0LH.
T: 01239 710 432 www.cawscenarth.co.uk
Award-winning, family-run business with a six generation tradition of cheese making.

WINE

VINTAGE ROOTS WINE MERCHANTS
Holdshott Farm, Reading Road, Heckfield, Hook, RG27 0JZ.
T: 08009 804 992 E: info@vintageroots.co.uk
www.vintageroots.co.uk
Award-winning organic wine suppliers, individually tasted and selected by Vintage Roots.

AL DENTE
Al dente describes vegetables that are cooked to the 'tender crisp' phase - still offering resistance to the bite, but cooked through. Al dente can also describe cooked pasta which is firm but not hard.

BAIN-MARIE
A pan or other container of hot water with a bowl placed on top of it. This allows the steam from the water to heat the bowl so ingredients can be gently heated or melted.

BEURRE NOISETTE
Unsalted butter is melted over a low heat until it begins to caramelise and brown. When it turns a nutty colour, it should be removed from the heat to stop it burning. Can be used as a base for butter sauces or added to cakes and batters.

BLANCH
Boiling an ingredient before removing it and plunging it in ice cold water in order to stop the cooking process.

CARTOUCHE
A piece of greaseproof paper that covers the surface of a stew, soup, stock or sauce to reduce evaporation.

CHINOIS
A conical sieve with an extremely fine mesh. It is used to strain custards, purées, soups and sauces, producing a very smooth texture.

CLARIFIED BUTTER
Milk fat rendered from butter to separate the milk solids and water from the butter fat.

CONFIT
A method of cooking where the meat is cooked and submerged in a liquid to add flavour. Often this liquid is rendered fat. Confit can also apply to fruits - fruit confits are cooked and preserved in sugar, the result is like candied fruits.

DEGLAZE
To make a gravy or sauce by adding liquid to the cooking juices and food particles in a pan in which meat or other ingredients have been cooked.

EMULSION/EMULSIFY
In the culinary arts, an emulsion is a mixture of two liquids that would ordinarily not mix together, like oil and vinegar.

GLOSSARY

FRENCH TRIMMED

To French trim, fat, meat or skin is cut away to expose a piece of bone, so that it sticks out.

It also means that any excess fat is cut off. French Trimming can be done to lamb chops and bigger cuts; it can even can be done to chicken legs or breasts.

GASTRIQUE

A caramelised sugar, deglazed with vinegar, used as a flavouring for sauces.

JULIENNE

A culinary knife cut in which the vegetable is sliced into long thin strips, similar to matchsticks.

LIQUOR

The liquid that is left over from the cooking of meat or vegetables. Can be incorporated into sauces and gravy.

MACERATED

Raw, dried or preserved fruit and vegetables soaked in a liquid to soften the food or to absorb the flavour.

MIREPOIX

Finely diced combination of celery (pascal, celery or celeriac), onions and carrots. There are many regional mirepoix variations, which can sometimes be just one of these ingredients, or include additional spices creating a rich, flavoursome base to sauces or stews.

NAGE

A term for a flavoured liquid used for poaching delicate foods, typically seafood. A traditional nage is a broth flavoured with white wine, vegetables and herbs, in which seafood is poached. The liquid is then reduced and thickened with cream and/or butter.

PANE

To coat with flour, beaten egg and breadcrumbs for deep frying.

QUENELLE

A neat, three-sided oval (resembling a mini rugby ball) that is formed by gently smoothing the mixture between two dessert spoons.

SABAYON

Made by beating egg yolks with a liquid over simmering water until thickened and increased in volume. The liquid can be water, but Champagne or wine is often used.

SAUTE

To fry in a small amount of fat.

SOUS VIDE

French for 'under vacuum.' A method of cooking food sealed in airtight plastic bags in a water bath or in a temperature-controlled steam environment for longer than normal cooking times. The intention is to cook the item evenly, ensuring that the inside is properly cooked without overcooking the outside, and to retain moisture.

ALL THE INGREDIENTS FOR YOUR RECIPE TO SUCCESS

Relish is proud to have worked with more than 1500 of the UK's finest chefs to showcase their wonderful restaurants and food but there is a huge appetite for more.

Jean Christophe Novelli and Mark Greenaway are just two of the industry's leading lights who worked with our small, professional and dedicated team to produce their own beautiful books - stamped with their personality and signature dishes.

As an independent publisher, we focus on you, your restaurant and your region to showcase culinary excellence to our readers who are always hungry to try out new dishes.

Owning this book is just for starters, reading it is the main course. Why not go for dessert and let us help you create a bespoke publication of your own to share with your loyal customers and attract new fans along the way?

You will be on the shelves alongside our fantastic portfolio of beautifully illustrated guides, which are stocked nationally in Waterstones, Harvey Nichols, in each featured restaurant, in leading independent stores and online globally.

Relish has a small, friendly, professional team, with experience in publishing, print management, editing, proofing, photography, design and artwork, sales distribution and marketing. We ensure a personal approach, working exceptionally hard to develop a great product which reflects each chef's talent and passion.

Duncan and Teresa Peters established the company in 2009, with a vision of building a niche publishing house for food lovers. The success of Relish Publications is reflected in the fact that we are the UK's leading regional recipe book publisher.

To book a personal consultation with our friendly, dedicated team contact our head office on 01670 571 635.

"Relish books are full of enjoyable recipes and ideas for making the most edible treasures we have on our doorstep; both places to eat them and new, exciting ways to cook them."

Angela Hartnett, MBE

"The Relish cookbook offers the home cook some great inspiration to make the most of these wonderful ingredients in season."

Tom Kitchin

"With mouth-watering, easy to follow recipes and beautiful photography, this book is a must have for any foodie, from professional chef to the inspired home cook."

Michael Caines MBE

The North East and Yorkshire has an amazing food and drink scene with a fantastic array of produce and restaurants - available on your doorstep. Relish gives you a taste of what we all have to offer through the pages of this superb book."

Kenny Atkinson

"Relish Midlands is a fantastic recipe book that brings together so many of the talented chefs and quality restaurants in the area. It gives you a taste of what our exciting region has to offer as well as the encouragement to try some new recipes."

Adam Stokes

"Relish Wales is a fabulous way to showcase some of our beautiful country's fabulous eateries and to be able to share our food with a wider audience."

Stephen Terry

AVAILABLE TO BUY IN OUR FEATURED RESTAURANTS & IN ALL GOOD BOOKSHOPS

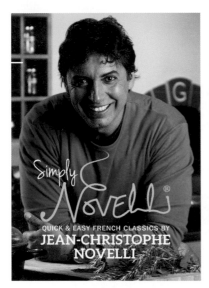

Simply Novelli
QUICK & EASY FRENCH CLASSICS BY
JEAN-CHRISTOPHE NOVELLI

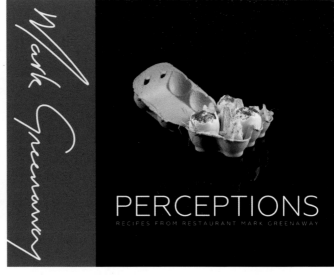

Mark Greenaway

PERCEPTIONS
RECIPES FROM RESTAURANT MARK GREENAWAY

Relish
WALES

Original recipes from the region's finest chefs and restaurants. Introduction by chef Will Holland.

Relish
SOUTH EAST

Original recipes from the region's finest chefs and restaurants. Introduction by Angela Hartnett, MBE.

Relish
SCOTLAND
THIRD HELPING

Original recipes from the region's finest chefs and restaurants. Featuring the Michelin starred chefs of Scotland.

Relish
NORTH EAST & YORKSHIRE
SECOND HELPING
Original recipes from the North East and Yorkshire's finest chefs and restaurants. Introduction by Kenny Atkinson.

Relish
SOUTH WEST
Original recipes from the South West's finest chefs and restaurants. Introduction by Michael Caines MBE.

Relish
WALES
SECOND HELPING
Original recipes from the region's finest chefs and restaurants. Introduction by James Sommerin.

Relish
NORTH WEST
Original recipes from the region's finest chefs and restaurants. Introduction by Paul Heathcote, MBE.

Relish
SOUTH WEST
SECOND HELPING
Original recipes from the South West's finest chefs and restaurants. Introduction by chef Nathan Outlaw.

Relish
MIDLANDS
SECOND HELPING
Original recipes from the region's finest chefs and restaurants. Introduction by Adam Stokes.

CONVERSION CHART

COOKING TEMPERATURES

Degrees Celsius	Fahrenheit	Gas Mark
140	275	1
150	300	2
160-170	325	3
180	350	4
190	375	5
200-210	400	6
220	425	7
230	450	8
240	475	9

*Temperatures for fan-assisted ovens are, as a general rule, normally about 20°C lower than regular oven temperature.

WEIGHT MEASUREMENT CONVERSIONS

1 teaspoon (5ml/5g)	$^1/_4$ oz
1 tablespoon (15ml/15g)	$^3/_4$ oz
10g	$^1/_2$ oz
25g	1oz
50g	2oz
75g	3oz
150g	5oz
200g	7oz
250g	9oz
350g	12oz
450g	1lb
1kg	2.2lb

VOLUME MEASUREMENT CONVERSIONS

55ml	2 fl oz
150ml	$^1/_4$ pt
275ml	$^1/_2$ pt
570ml	1 pt
1 litre	$1^3/_4$ pt